SOCRATES, BUDDHA, CONFUCIUS, JESUS

Other works available in English translation

THE FUTURE OF MANKIND

THE IDEA OF THE UNIVERSITY

TRUTH AND SYMBOL

MAN IN THE MODERN AGE

REASON AND EXISTENZ

THE ORIGIN AND GOAL OF HISTORY,

TRAGEDY IS NOT ENOUGH

REASON AND ANTI-REASON IN OUR TIME

THE WAY TO WISDOM

THE PERENNIAL SCOPE OF PHILOSOPHY

THE QUESTION OF GERMAN GUILT

KARL JASPERS

SOCRATES, BUDDHA, CONFUCIUS, JESUS

The Paradigmatic Individuals

EDITED BY HANNAH ARENDT

TRANSLATED BY RALPH MANHEIM

A Harvest Book

A Helen and Kurt Wolff Book

Harcourt, Brace & World, Inc., New York

ISBN   0-15-683580-0

D.6.70

Originally published in German as part of
Die grossen Philosophen I
by R. Piper & Co. Verlag, München, 1957

Acknowledgments

Acknowledgment is made for permission to use the following: For the quotations from Arthur Waley, *Three Ways of Thought in Ancient China*, London, Allen and Unwin, 1939. For the quotations from *Buddhism in Translations*, ed. by Henry Clarke Warren (Harvard Oriental Series, Vol. 3), Harvard University Press, Cambridge, Mass.

CONTENTS

JESUS

Considerations Regarding the Paradigmatic Individuals

SOCRATES, BUDDHA, CONFUCIUS, JESUS

The four paradigmatic individuals have exerted a historical influence of incomparable scope and depth. Other men of great stature may have been equally important for smaller groups. But when it comes to broad, enduring influence over many hundreds of years, they are so far above all others that they must be singled out if we are to form a clear view of the world's history.

No single type can account for these four men. Their historicity and consequent uniqueness can be perceived only within the all-embracing historicity of humanity, which in each of them expresses itself in a wholly different way. To discover this common root has been possible only since mankind has achieved a unity of communication and the different cultures have learned of each other's crucial individuals. In an earlier day, each one was the only crucial individual for large parts of mankind, and as a matter of fact has remained so even since the others became known.

SOCRATES

1. LIFE (469–399 B.C.)

Socrates' father was a stonemason, his mother a midwife. But despite this undistinguished birth, he was a citizen of Athens. Living frugally, he was materially independent, thanks to a small inheritance and the state subsidies that were paid out to all Athenians (theater fees and the like). In fulfillment of his military duties, he fought as a hoplite in the Peloponnesian War, taking part in the engagements at Delion and Amphipolis. In line with his compulsory political duties, he served as chairman of the council in 406 and sought to obtain justice in opposition to the enraged mob which demanded and obtained the execution of the generals who had commanded the Athenian troops at the battle of Arginusae. But he never aspired to any important position in the state or the army. His wife Xanthippe was of no importance in his life as a philosopher.

Interestingly enough, we know how Socrates looked. He is the first philosopher to stand before us in the flesh. He was an ugly man, with bulging eyes. His stub nose, thick lips, big belly, and squat build suggest a Silenus or satyr. He was gifted with a rugged constitution, inured to cold and hardship.

The Socrates of our portrait is a middle-aged man. We know next to nothing of his youth. He grew up in the powerful, prosperous, brilliant Athens that issued from the Persian wars. He was almost forty at the outbreak of the disastrous Peloponnesian War (431), and it was only then that he became a public figure. The earliest document that speaks of him is the *Clouds* of Aristophanes, which makes fun of him (423). He experienced the decline and defeat of Athens (405). At the age of seventy he was accused of impiety, tried, and condemned to death. He died in 399 by drinking hemlock.

2. INTELLECTUAL DEVELOPMENT

His intellectual development can only be inferred. He knew the nature philosophy of Anaxagoras and Archelaus. He experienced the coming of the

Sophists and mastered their method. Neither of these philosophies satisfied him. Natural philosophy was of no help to a man's soul. The Sophists, to be sure, accomplished a great deal by making things questionable. But in so doing they made the mistake either of setting up a supposedly new knowledge or of denying the validity of all tradition. Amid these cross-currents of thought Socrates had no new doctrine, nor did he lay claim to any self-sufficient method.

One day Socrates must have come to a turning point. When he saw that natural philosophy had no bearing on man's serious problems, when he recognized the demoralizing tendency of Sophism, he did not know the truth as something definite and different. But he was filled with an aware-ness of his vocation, of a divine mission. Like the Prophets, he was certain of his calling; unlike them, he had nothing to proclaim. No God had chosen him to tell men what He commanded. His mission was only to search in the company of men, himself a man among men. To question un-relentingly, to expose every hiding place. To demand no faith in anything or in himself, but to demand thought, questioning, testing, and so refer man to his own self. But since man's self resides solely in the knowledge of the true and the good, only the man who takes such thinking seriously, who is determined to be guided by the truth, is truly himself.

3. THE DIALOGUE

The Socratic dialogue was the fundamental reality of this life: he conversed with artisans, statesmen, artists, Sophists, harlots. Like many Athenians he spent his life in the street, the market place, the gymnasia, or at banquets. It was a life of conversation with everyone. Conversation was the free Athenian's form of life, but now, as the instrument of Socratic philosophiz-ing, it became something different: a conversation that aroused, disturbed, compelled men's innermost souls. Conversation, dialogue, is necessary for the truth itself, which by its very nature opens up to an individual only in dialogue with another individual. To achieve clarity Socrates needed men, and he was convinced that they needed him: above all, the young men. Socrates wanted to educate.

What he meant by education was not some casual operation that the knower performs on the unknowing, but the element in which men, com-municating with each other, come to themselves, in which the truth opens up to them. The young men helped him when he wanted to help them. He taught them to discover the difficulties in the seemingly self-evident; he con-fused them, forced them to think, to search, to inquire over and over again, and not to sidestep the answer, and this they could bear because they were convinced that truth is what joins men together. From this basic reality there developed, after Socrates' death, the prose poetry of the dialogues, whose master was Plato.

Socrates did not, like Plato after him, attack Sophism as a whole. He founded no party, made no propaganda, justified nothing, established no school or institution. He developed no program of state reform, no system of knowledge. He did not address his remarks to any particular public or to the popular assembly. "I always address the individual," he says in the *Apology,* and ironically explains that since no one who speaks frankly and openly to a crowd is sure of his life, a champion of justice who wishes to remain alive even a little while had better speak only to individuals. This argument can be taken in a deeper sense. The untruth of the present state of affairs, regardless of whether the form of government is democratic or aristocratic or tyrannical, cannot be remedied by great political actions. No improvement is possible unless the individual is educated by educating himself, unless his hidden being is awakened to reality through an insight which is at the same time inner action, a knowledge which is at the same time virtue. He who becomes a true man becomes a true citizen.

But apart from his success and usefulness in the state, the individual is important for his own sake. The independence that comes of self-mastery (*eukrateia*), the true freedom which grows with knowledge—these are the ultimate foundations on which a man can face the godhead.

4. THE SUBSTANCE OF THE SOCRATIC LIFE

If philosophy is "doctrine," Socrates is not a philosopher. If the history of Greek philosophy is taken as a history of theoretical positions, he has no place in it. The significance of Socrates' approach is that one must know one's ignorance and embark on the journey of thought. Socrates knew the boundary line where demonstration stops but where, in the presence of questioning, the substance in which it is rooted stands fast and burns all the more brightly.

This substance is Socrates' piety. It is made up, first, of his trust that the truth will disclose itself if one perseveres in questioning; that through a candid awareness of what one does not know, one will arrive not at nothingness but at the knowledge that is crucial for life; second, of his belief in the gods and the divinity of the polis; third, of his confidence in his daimonion.

A. While discussing virtue (*aretē*) with Socrates, Meno (in Plato's dialogue) is driven into a corner by Socrates' questions. "Even before I met you," says Meno, "they told me that in plain truth you are a perplexed man yourself and reduce others to perplexity. At this moment I feel you are exerting magic and witchcraft upon me and positively laying me under your spell until I am just a mass of helplessness. If I may be flippant . . . you are exactly like the flat sting ray that one meets in the sea. Whenever anyone comes into contact with it, it numbs him. . . . If you behaved like this as a foreigner in another country, you would most likely be arrested as a wizard." Whereupon Socrates: "If the sting ray paralyzes others only through being paralyzed itself, then the comparison is just, but not otherwise. It is not that, knowing the answer myself, I perplex other people. The truth is rather that I infect them also with the perplexity I feel myself." In the same state of mind Theaetetus says that he feels dizzy; and Socrates replies that this is the beginning of philosophy.

From perplexity grows insight. In the *Meno* this is shown by a parable: a certain slave is confident at first that he knows the answer to a mathematical question; then he gets into difficulties and recognizes his ignorance, until at length, through further questions, he arrives at the correct solution. As this example shows, truth comes to us in dialogue. It is still unknown to both participants, but it is there. Both of them circle around it and are guided by it.

Socrates wished to start men searching, but in their searching he wished them to be confident of finding. He likened (*Theaetetus*) this activity of his to the midwife's art. Theaetetus knows no answer, thinks himself incapable of finding one. "And yet," he says, "I cannot shake off the desire." "You have labor pains," says Socrates, "because you are not empty but ready to bring forth." And Socrates goes on to describe his way of speaking with the young men. Like a midwife he ascertains whether there is pregnancy or not; his methods enable him to provoke pains and to appease them; he knows how to distinguish true birth from the birth of a vain shadow, a counterfeit. He himself, he admits, is barren of wisdom and those who accuse him of merely questioning are right. For "the god compels me to be a midwife, but does not allow me to give birth." At first those who converse with him simply seem to become more ignorant, but only because they are freed from pseudo knowledge. Then "if the god is gracious to them, they all make astonishing progress . . . yet it is quite clear that they never learned anything from me. . . . But to me and the god they owe their delivery."

Socrates does not hand down wisdom but makes the other find it. The other thinks he knows, but Socrates makes him aware of his ignorance, so leading him to find authentic knowledge in himself. From miraculous depths this man raises up what he already knew, but without knowing that he knew it. This means that each man must find knowledge in himself; it is not a commodity that can be passed from hand to hand, but can only be awakened. When it comes to light, it is like a recollection of something known long ago. And that is why, in the pursuit of philosophy, I can search without knowing. A Sophist had said: I can search only for what I know; if I know it, I no longer have to search for it; if I do not know it, I cannot search for it. In the Socratic view, however, to philosophize is to search for what I already know. But I know it unconsciously, as though in a dim, ancient memory, and now I wish to know it in the bright light of my present consciousness.

Thus Socrates' questioning, disproving, testing are sustained by the confidence that by forthright thinking a man, with God's help, will arrive at the truth. Not by vain thinking in words, but by the meaningful thinking that springs from the source. Hence the confidence.

B. Socrates believed in the traditional gods; he sacrificed to them, obeyed the authority of Delphi, took part in the festivals. This religion, which told the Greeks what not to do and not to will, and from which all willing and thinking drew their meaning, could be watered down or evaded, and this is what many of the Sophists did. Or else one could live in it, observe it with veneration, find in it the ground without which everything is groundless. That is what Socrates did. Hence the magnificent, self-conscious "naïveté" with which Socrates lived in the tradition of a self-evident truth grounded in history and springing uncomprehended from the depths of being. Where your own insight brings no decision, it is best to follow the religion of the fathers, the laws of the state.

Socrates was inseparably attached to his native state, the state of Solon, the Persian wars, Pericles. It was a state built on a legality established in times immemorial and continuously reinforced, without which its life would have been unthinkable. This accounts for Socrates' fidelity to the law. In the trial following the battle of Arginusae, he refused to put the verdict to a vote, because under the existing conditions such a procedure was illegal. He refused to escape from prison, to break the laws which remained valid as laws, even though they had served as a framework for injustice. Nothing could alter this attitude. The tyranny of the Thirty forbade him to teach, the democracy put him to death. He belonged to no party. But he held unswervingly to the idea of law in the historical form of the Athenian polis. It is unthinkable that Socrates, who spoke only to individuals, who took personal responsibility as an absolute, who subjected everything to critical examination, should ever, like Alcibiades, have made the state a tool of his personal ambition, much less taken up arms against the city in which he was born. Nor was he willing to become an uprooted citizen of the world. It would never have occurred to him to emigrate, to Sicily like Aeschylus or to Macedonia like Euripides, old men embittered against their own country. He knew beyond a question that his existence was inseparable from Athens. In Plato's *Apology,* Socrates, when offered the choice between exile and death, chooses death: "A fine life that would be for me at my age, to leave my country and wander from one city to another for the rest of my days." In the *Crito,* Socrates imagines that the laws have come to question him and in this passage discloses his attitude toward them: it is thanks to the laws that he was born in legitimate wedlock, an Athenian citizen, and that his father was able to bring him up. He has demonstrated his support of the laws by refusing to leave Athens, by preferring death to banishment at his trial. He does not set himself up as their equal but acknowledges his obligation to obey them. He must submit to the sentence of the judges as a citizen submits to the order that sends him off to war. He is no more entitled to lift his hand against his country than against his father and mother, even if he believes that he has been treated unjustly.

This distinguishes Socrates from the Sophists. Though his mercilessly critical questioning may make him seem one of them, he never departs from his historical foundations but piously recognizes the laws of the polis and thoughtfully examines their meaning. First I must affirm the ground on which I stand, from which I come, which at all times remains present to me, without which I slip into nothingness.

This is what is memorable and characteristic in Socrates: he carries his criticism to the extreme, yet never ceases to recognize an absolute authority which may be called the true, the good, or reason. For him this authority represents an absolute responsibility. To whom? He does not know, but he speaks of gods. Whatever may happen in reality, this is his fixed point, which stands fast in a world of endless change.

But when evil befalls him, when injustice strikes, when his own polis destroys him, he lives by the maxim that it is better to suffer than to commit injustice. Socrates knows no rebellion against his state, against world and God. He does not inquire into the source of evil as though God required justification. He goes to his death without revolt and without defiance. He knew neither the despair that comes of questioning divine justice nor any comforting answer to the question, but drew unfailing composure from his belief in a self-evident justice. No matter how the benefits of fortune are distributed in the world, only one thing matters: to live according to the norm of truth, which is elucidated in thought. Those who wish a guarantee, a certainty, a credo in regard to God, immortality, the end of all things, will not get it from Socrates. The essential for man is to risk living as though he knew the good exists. Nonknowledge guides me over and over again to the point where I am myself because I recognize the good as the true, and where it is entirely up to me to live in accordance with it.

c. What should be done in the concrete, unique situation cannot always, in Socrates' view, be decided by reason. The gods come to our help. This help is a limit beyond which there can only be obedience without understanding. Socrates tells of the daimonion that has spoken to him at crucial moments ever since his childhood. This voice ". . . always forbids but never commands me to do anything I am going to do." This voice, for example, said no whenever he thought of going into political life. When students who had left him wished to resume their relation with him, the daimonion expressed its opposition in some cases, but not in others. During his trial the voice was silent and this he found strange and encouraging. "Recently the divine faculty . . . has constantly been . . . opposing me even about trifles, if I was going to make a slip or error in any matter; and now as you see there has come upon me that which may be thought . . . the last and worst evil [the death sentence]. But the divine voice made no sign of opposition, either when I was leaving my house in the morning, or when I was on my way to the court, or when I was speaking . . . the customary sign would surely have opposed me had I been going to evil and not to good" (*Apology*). "Before me," says Socrates, "I doubt if anyone was ever favored with a warning voice of this kind" (*Republic*).

The voice brings no knowledge. It suggests no definite action. It merely says no. It forbids him to say or do anything that would have evil consequences. And Socrates obeys its prohibitions without attempting to understand them. It is not an objective authority but incommunicable. It applies only to the actions of Socrates himself, not to those of others. He cannot invoke it as a justification but can only accept it as a hint.

Daimonion (Demon??)

5. THE TRIAL

The life of Socrates was not dramatic, except for its end. His trial for blasphemy ended with the death sentence. This outcome was no accident, a long history led up to it. In the *Clouds* (423) Aristophanes portrays a Socrates who engages in natural philosophy, concerns himself with celestial phenomena and the things under the earth, denies the traditional gods, for which he substitutes the air and the clouds, teaches the art of arguing a cause even if it is unjust, and takes money for his teaching—all the exact opposite of Socrates as we know him. Since then, new accusations had been raised. He was accused of teaching the young men idleness, of basing criminal doctrines on his interpretation of the poets, of numbering such enemies of the people as Alcibiades and Critias among his students. What gave rise to this astonishingly false picture? As a young man, to be sure, he had concerned himself with natural philosophy and Sophism, but above all he was regarded as the representative of the whole new philosophical movement, which was opposed by public opinion. The people confused the man who had transcended Sophism with Sophism itself. For the new method by which he refuted it was intolerable. Socrates questioned unremittingly; he drove his listeners to the basic problems of man, but did not solve them. Confusion, a consciousness of inferiority, and the demands he raised created anger and hatred. One such reaction is that of Hippias: For you always "mock at others, questioning and examining everybody, and are never willing to render an account of yourself or to state an opinion about anything" (Xenophon). And so Socrates, in the year 399, was tried on charges "of violating the laws, for he does not believe in the gods of our country, of observing a faith in a new kind of demon, and of leading the youth astray."

Socrates seems to have ignored these accusations for years. As long as he lived, there was no literature in defense of his philosophy. He himself never wrote a line. He had not withdrawn into aristocratic seclusion, nor limited his teaching to a select coterie, but had taught in the streets and market place, in full public view. Even though he conversed only with individuals, he left the Athenians no peace.

The God, says Socrates—and this is the main point in his defense—had bidden him to spend his life delving into himself and other men. "I shall obey the God rather than you, and while I have life and strength I shall never cease from the practice of philosophy, exhorting anyone whom I meet and saying to him after my manner: You, my friend . . . are you not ashamed . . . to care so little about wisdom and truth and the greatest improvement of the soul, which you never regard or heed at all?"

And his defense turns into an attack on the judges. "For if you kill me," he declares, "you will not easily find another like me, who, if I may use such a ludicrous figure of speech, am a sort of gadfly, given to the city by God . . . always fastening upon you, arousing and persuading and reproaching you. . . . [But] you may feel out of temper like a person suddenly awakened from sleep and might suddenly strike me dead . . . and then sleep on for the remainder of your lives."

His death more than anything else fashioned the image of Socrates that passed into tradition. He is the martyr of philosophy, victim of a judicial murder at the hands of the Athenian democracy. Yet some have questioned this condemnation of his judges. Their argument is roughly as follows: Socrates might easily have saved himself by offering the right kind of defense. In overweening defiance of human authority, he insulted his judges. He was offered a number of ways out and failed to take advantage of them. He might easily have avoided execution by escaping. He refused to make his peace with the unwritten conventions of the community. He willfully brought about his own death. Hence it was not a judicial murder but a judicial suicide. Those who take such a view, who hold that not the murderer but the victim was guilty, fail to see that his divine mission to work for the truth forbade Socrates to lose himself in servile acceptance of the prevailing untruth. He was a true martyr, that is to say, a witness.

These arguments against the thesis of a judicial murder are of interest for our judgment not of Socrates but of the reader of the Socratic texts. Like everything Socrates did, his defense presents dangers to our understanding; it is valid only in conjunction with his philosophy. Considered in the abstract, it teaches the reader a false attitude of revolt, defiance, the wrong kind of edification. Instead of entering into Socrates' fundamental state of mind, the reader himself, by involuntarily regarding Socrates as presumptuous, becomes arrogant and presumptuous himself. He derives pleasure from what he takes for an insult to the people and the judges. He makes the mistake of deriving universal rules from Socrates' apology, of making it an abstract model. Only one who thought like Socrates could, without falsehood, act and die like Socrates. Even Plato would not have died like Socrates.

Another view is that first presented by Hegel: Athens was right, for it was defending its substance; Socrates was right, for he was ushering in a new era, which presupposed the destruction of that substance. Such absolutizing of history and aesthetic objectivization of a tragic conflict seems utterly inappropriate to an event such as Socrates. Of course each era has its own spirit, and immense transformations have taken place from era to era. But this does not mean that each era has its own absolute justice and that consequently there are many justices. Through all the eras runs something that is valid for men as men. What men do stands before a higher court than that of history. What is true and good, what is false and vile ought not to be veiled or exorcised as tragedy.

It is only through Socrates himself that we can reconcile ourselves to his death. He died without defiance or blame. "I am not angry with my condemners or my accusers"—this was his last word. He was convinced that for a good man there can be no evil; his cause will not be neglected by the gods.

But his next to last words were: "I tell you who have killed me, that immediately after my departure punishment . . . will come upon you. . . . There will be more accusers of you than there are now; accusers whom hitherto I have restrained; and as they are younger, they will be more inconsiderate with you and more dangerous. If you think that by killing men you can prevent someone from censuring your evil lives, you are mistaken."

6. THE PLATONIC TRANSFIGURATION
OF SOCRATES

The picture of Socrates in Plato's dialogues is not a historically accurate record of scenes, conversations, sayings. But though it is not a record, it is not mere invention. What Plato invented was invented in the spirit of reality, the reality of this mysterious thinker who knows no parallel. The whole picture, as it unfolds in all its aspects, is the transfigured reality itself. There is no point in examining such a reality for its philological, photographic accuracy. One who denies the historic reality cannot be convinced by proofs. It took Plato to see and communicate the reality of Socrates. What Plato saw we may see through him and with him: Socrates before his death (*Apology, Crito, Phaedo*) and in life (*Symposium, Phaedrus*).

The death of Socrates gives a picture of serene composure in nonknowledge filled with ineffable certainty.

Nonknowledge is the ground and end of all speaking about death. Socrates says: Those who fear death imagine that they know what no one knows. Perhaps it is the greatest good fortune and they fear it as though they knew it was the greatest of evils. The possibilities can be appraised: either death is equivalent to nothingness, without sensation of anything at all, like a dreamless sleep; then all eternity seems no longer than a single night. Or else death is the migration of the soul to another place, where all the dead are gathered, where righteous judges speak the truth, where we shall meet with those who have been unjustly sentenced and done to death, where men live on in dialogue, still seeking to ascertain who is wise, and where we shall enjoy the indescribable bliss of speaking with the best of men. Whatever the truth about death may be, for a good man there is no evil, neither in life nor in death.

In demonstrating the immortality of the soul, "which is beyond any doubt," Socrates seems to be saying that all peace of mind is based on such certainty. However, freedom from doubt has its source in righteous action and in the search for truth. The "proofs" come afterward. A certainty based on rational proof is no secure possession, and indeed, Socrates speaks expressly of the "venture" of living in the hope of immortality. For ideas of immortality form "a fully justified faith, worthy that we venture to devote ourselves to it. For the venture is beautiful and peace of mind demands such ideas, which work like magic incantations." But to guard against any certainty that might be regarded as a possession conferred by knowledge, Socrates, with unchanging serenity, revives a doubt. "If what I say is true, then I do well to be persuaded of the truth; but if there be nothing after death, still, during the short time that remains, I shall not distress my friends with lamentations, and my ignorance will not last."

Crito asks Socrates how he wishes to be buried. "In any way you like," he replies. "But you must get hold of me, and take care that I do not run away from you." Then he smiles serenely and says: "I cannot make Crito believe that I am the true Socrates who has been talking and conducting the argument; he fancies that I am the other Socrates whom he will soon see, a dead body. But say that you are burying my body only, and do with that whatever is usual, and what you think best." The mood of Socrates' friends in these hours before his death is strangely compounded of buoyancy and despair. In grief and an incomprehensible elation they peer into a mysterious reality.

For Socrates, there is nothing tragic about death. "You, Simmias, and Cebes, and the others, will depart at some time or other. Me already, as a tragic poet would say, the voice of fate calls." In other words, the time of death has become a matter of indifference. Socrates is above death.

He forbids his friends to mourn. "One must leave this earth in reverent peace. Be quiet and have patience." For Socrates seeks companionship in quiet truth; lamentation is not a bond among men. He gently dismisses Xanthippe, he has no heart for wailing. It is thought, as long as it is granted him, that exalts a man's soul, not heedless surrender to grief. True, we men are assailed by grief in our lives, and we lament. But in the end lamentation must cease, giving way to peace and acceptance of our lot. Socrates sets the great example: where consuming sorrow seems in place, there springs the great, loving peace which opens the soul. Death has lost its meaning. It is not veiled over, but the authentic life is not a life toward death; it is a life toward the good.

While Socrates, in his last moments, already seems far away from life, still, he is lovingly aware of every little human reality, such as the jailer's kind attentiveness. He has a thought for the proprieties: "Perhaps it will be well to bathe before drinking the poison, and so spare the women the trouble of washing my body."

All pathos vanishes amid jests and such attention to practical matters. These betoken peace of mind. Democritus, who remained more on the surface of things, believed that to achieve peace of mind it sufficed to live with moderation and stick to the tasks that are within your capacities. He did not know the inner upheavals which once illuminated gave Socrates a deeper, wiser peace of mind. What made Socrates free was that in non-knowledge he had certainty of the goal toward which he had undertaken the venture of his whole life and now of his death.

The *Phaedo,* along with the *Apology* and the *Crito,* is among the few irreplaceable documents of mankind. All through antiquity men of philosophical mind read it and learned how to die at peace by accepting their lot, however cruel and unjust.

The apparently cool equanimity of this attitude is, however, deceptive. Actually, we cannot read these dialogues without becoming engulfed by deep emotion which affects also our thinking. Here we find an imperative without fanaticism, the highest aspiration without ethical dogma. Keep yourself open for the one absolute. Until you achieve it, do not throw yourself away, for in it you can live and die at peace.

Though we see him clearly, Plato's Socrates is a mysterious figure and the mystery extends even to the physical man. His indestructible health inured him to privation and excess alike. After drinking all night he carries on a profound philosophical discussion with Aristophanes and Agathon. When both his companions have fallen asleep, he stands up and leaves. "He went to the Lyceum where he took a bath and passed the day as usual. In the evening he retired to rest at his own home." But he can act very oddly. Walking with a friend, he stops still, deep in thought. He could stand that way all night, staring into space. When dawn came, "he made a prayer to the sun and went his way." He is as ugly as a Silenus yet exerts an almost magical attraction. Strange (*atopos*), unfathomable, this man cannot be reduced to any norm. Everything he is and says always seems to have more than one meaning.

In the *Symposium* Plato puts a description of Socrates into the mouth of

Alcibiades, a noble youth whose drunkenness has freed him from all restraint. Carried away by a love that he himself was powerless to understand, this young man who in his life was untrue to Socrates speaks of him as follows: "I declare that he bears a strong resemblance to the figures of Silenus in the statuaries' shops; they are hollow inside and when they are taken apart, they contain images of gods.

"The mere fragments of your words amaze and possess the souls of every man. And if I were not afraid you would think me hopelessly drunk, I would have sworn as well as spoken to the influence they have always had and still have over me. For my heart leaps within me more than that of any Corybantian reveller, and my eyes rain tears when I hear them. I have heard Pericles and other great orators, and I thought they spoke well, but I never had any such feeling that I could hardly endure the life which I am leading. He makes me confess that I ought not to live as I do, neglecting the wants of my own soul and engaging in public life; therefore I hold my ears and tear myself away from him. He is the only person who ever made me ashamed. Many a time I should be glad for him to vanish from the face of the earth, but I know that, if that were to happen, my sorrow would far outweigh my relief.

"None of you know him; but I will reveal him to you. See you how fond he is of the fair? He is always with them and always being smitten by them. But that is only his outer mask, like the hollowed head of the Silenus. But when he is opened, what temperance there is within. Know you that beauty and wealth and honor at which the many wonder, are of no account with him, and are utterly despised by him; he regards not at all the persons who are gifted with them; mankind are nothing to him; all his life is spent in mocking and flouting them. But when I opened him and looked within at his serious purpose, I saw in him divine and golden images of such fascinating beauty that I was ready to do in a moment whatever Socrates commanded."

Xenophon's simple portrait is very different from this transfiguration, but there is no contradiction in the essentials. Xenophon sees particulars and disconnected ideas; he sees a sturdy, able man full of wisdom and understanding; he sets out to examine Socrates' faults as fairly as his virtues, but he can find no faults. Plato goes to the very center of the Socratic essence, which can only be pictured metaphorically; taking its manifestations as symbols, he arrives at a limit where judgment abdicates in the presence of the extraordinary. Xenophon is informed; he communicates Socrates by giving us all the data he can collect. But Plato is captivated; in him Socrates called forth a movement which transformed his whole life and it is only through this movement that he discloses the reality and truth of Socrates. For both Plato and Xenophon, Socrates is human; neither deifies him; but in Xenophon, the man himself with his possible truth is a rational-ethical being who can be fully known and understood, while in Plato he is a man who speaks from inexhaustible depths, who springs from an unfathomable source and lives toward an unfathomable end.

7. INFLUENCE

The Socratic tradition bursts into being with his death. The terrible event moved his friends to speak of Socrates, to testify in his favor, to philosophize in the Socratic spirit. This was the beginning of the Socratic literature, whose greatest representative is Plato. Socrates' prediction was confirmed. His friends would leave the Athenians no peace. Although he had left no work, no doctrine, much less system, he gave impetus to the mightiest movement in Greek philosophy, a movement that has endured down to our own day.

But strange to say, his pupils did not see and communicate the same picture of Socrates. Not one school arose, but many. All took Socrates as their source, and a number of contradictory tendencies arose. Even the figure of Socrates took many forms. Only one thing is common to all these witnesses: the experience of having undergone a transformation through contact with Socrates. This diversity in the Socratic tradition began with his death and has never ceased; it explains why there is still disagreement about the reality of Socrates.

The one point in which the many Socrateses converge is Socratic thought. It is through thought that those who felt the impact of Socrates became different men. Through Socrates thought manifested itself with the highest claims, involving the greatest dangers. Contact with him inspired men to think; this was the experience of all the Socratics. But immediately after his death fragmentation set in; each one began to think in a different way. Each one seems to have supposed that he possessed Socratic thought, while no one had it. Is this not the source of the never-ending impulsion which has not reached its goal to this day but which at times has risen to an almost inconceivable intensity?

The Socratic schools are known to us. Xenophon merely records the externals, but they are characterized by the modes of thought they developed: the Megarians (Euclid) developed logic and eristics, pointed out important logical fallacies; one of the Megarians, Diodorus Cronus, discovered the anomalies inherent in the idea of possibility. The Elian School (Phaedo) carried out dialectical investigations. The Cynics (Antisthenes) chose the path of self-sufficiency and inner independence, denied the importance of education and culture. From them descended Diogenes of Sinope. The Cyrenaic School developed a system of ethics from nature and the idea of pleasure ("Hedonism"). Plato, who, thanks to his range, depth, and openness to development, transmitted the main stream of Socratic thinking to future generations, avoided all these one-sided interpretations that led nowhere. None of these philosophies is the philosophy of Socrates. Each of them is an image reflecting one of the many possibilities in his thinking.

In later generations, however, the images of Socrates came to conceal his reality, which barely shines through them. So it came about that nearly all the philosophers of antiquity, despite their hostility to one another, saw in Socrates an incarnation of the ideal philosopher. Down through the centuries his figure has been unique.

For the Church Fathers, Socrates was a great figure, a precursor of the Christian martyrs. Like them he died for his belief and like them he was accused of blasphemy against the traditional religion. He was even mentioned in the same breath as Christ. Socrates and Christ are together in their opposition to Greek religion (Justin). "There is only one Socrates" (Tatian). Origen finds common ground between Socrates and Jesus. Socrates' insight into nonknowledge prepares the way for faith (Theodoret). Socrates' self-knowledge is the way to knowledge of God. Socrates saw that man can approach the divine only with a pure spirit, untainted by earthly passions. He confessed his own ignorance. But because no clarity concerning the *summum bonum* can be gleaned from his disquisitions, because in every case he merely arouses our interest, and sets up an affirmation only to topple it over, let each man take from Socrates what meets his needs (Augustine).

Insofar as the first Christian centuries lived in the shadow of antiquity, they lived also with Socrates. In the Middle Ages his name lost its radiance. Here and there it was mentioned: Yehuda Halevi looked upon Socrates as the representative of the most perfect human wisdom, which, however, cannot gain access to the divine. With the Renaissance and the reappearance of independent philosophy, Socrates too was restored to life. Erasmus wrote: *"Sancte Socrates, ora pro nobis."* For Montaigne, Socratic thinking meant skepticism and naturalness, which implied above all knowing how to die with composure. For the Enlightenment, Socrates was the independent thinker, the champion of ethical freedom. For Mendelssohn he was the man of moral excellence, who had conceived the proofs of the existence of God and of immortality. But this was only a beginning. It was Kierkegaard who first found an original approach to Socrates and who, of all modern thinkers, arrived at the profoundest interpretation of Socrates, his irony and nonknowledge, and of his philosophizing, not as a communication of truth, but as a goad to look for the truth. Nietzsche looked on Socrates as the great adversary of the Greek tragic spirit, the intellectualist and founder of science who ruined the Greek view of the world. He struggled with Socrates as long as he lived: "Socrates is so close to me that I am almost always engaged in a struggle with him." The future destinies of philosophy are sure to be reflected in its attitude toward Socrates.

In retrospect we may say that Socrates, whose reality was known and at the same time not known at all, became a kind of vessel into which men and whole epochs projected their own ideals: he has been regarded as a humble, God-fearing Christian; a self-assured rationalist; a demonic genius; a prophet of humanity; and sometimes even as a political conspirator, concealing his plan to seize power beneath the mask of the philosopher. He was none of these.

Modern philological investigation has contributed something new. Since Schleiermacher scholars have tried to establish a reliable picture of Socrates, asking: What can we know of Socrates on the basis of the historical sources? Applying the methods of historical critique, they have tried to show us a Socrates shorn of poetry and legend.

Yet the results are far from adding up to a scientific and universally accepted picture of Socrates. Instead, we have a number of mutually contradictory images suggesting that a historical picture of Socrates may be altogether an impossibility. We try in vain to combine the critical reconstructions of Socrates. Each one of the "reconstructors" asserts or denies the value of Plato, Xenophon, Aristophanes, or Aristotle as a source. The most radical inference was drawn by Gigon: Since we have no historical account of Socrates, but only poetry; since there was never any written work by Socrates himself, it is impossible to reconstruct the philosophy of Socrates. Thus any attempt to solve the riddle of Socrates is a waste of time. Gigon recognizes, however, that it cannot have been entirely by accident that Socrates and none other should have been chosen by Aristophanes as the representative of a noxious philosophy compounded of natural science, enlightenment, and Sophism; that Socrates and not some other Sophist should have been executed in the year 399; and that in a body of literature remarkable for its stature and range, just Socrates should have been made into an image of the true philosopher. But why all this happened, says Gigon, we do not know. We must forgo a historical Socrates.

Nevertheless, we have attempts at critical combination, more or less in accordance with Schleiermacher's formula: "What can Socrates have been, in addition to what Xenophon tells us of him, that would not contradict the traits of character and the maxims of conduct which Xenophon definitely identifies as Socratic? And what must he have been to justify Plato in introducing him in his dialogues as he does?" But the scholars who persist in comparing and combining in the hope of arriving at a historical Socrates must put their trust in "historical feeling."

If we require science to be universal and compelling, science can give us nothing in this case. Either it concludes that a collection of arguments and anecdotes from various sources has been transferred to Socrates, or else it disavows its own character as science by claiming to discover more than critical methods can justify, and then the result is a multiplicity of incompatible images, each one supposedly critical, in other words a result that cannot be called scientific.

Then Socrates becomes: the precursor of Plato's philosophy, who discovered the way to the concept (Zeller after Aristotle); or no philosopher at all, but an ethical revolutionary, a prophet, the creator of an ethos of self-mastery and self-sufficiency, of human self-liberation (Heinrich Maier); or the Socrates of all Plato's dialogues, creator of the theory of Ideas, of Plato's doctrines of immortality and of the ideal state, in which case everything Plato says of him is the historical truth (Burnet, Taylor). In contrast to all these positions, Werner Jaeger comes to the question with a reasonable method: Socrates is something of all these, though certain definite limits can be imposed (in particular, the philosophical doctrines of the later Platonic dialogues, beginning with the theory of Ideas, should not be attributed to Socrates); there must, in Socrates himself, have been something that made possible all that was thought and written about him. Our starting point must be Socrates' extraordinary influence, of which we have direct testimony. Thus Jaeger starts from a solid basis in fact, but at the same time reaches out beyond philology taken as a strict science.

8. THE LASTING SIGNIFICANCE OF SOCRATES

After studying the tradition, each of us retains an image of Socrates. Despite all the shifting possibilities, despite all our avowed uncertainty, we are left with a picture of Socrates that strikes us as real and not as a poetic invention. Though our picture of him may lack scientific precision, he stands compellingly before our eyes with all the captivating power of his human personality. It is impossible not to form an image of the historic Socrates. What is more, some image of Socrates is indispensable to our philosophical thinking. Perhaps we may say that today no philosophical thought is possible unless Socrates is present, if only as a pale shadow. The way in which a man experiences Socrates is fundamental to his thinking.

The thought that began for us with Socrates is at once free and mysterious. From the outset naïve certainty ceased to be possible for those who had been initiated into his thinking. Liberated thought became its own great question. The striving to ground life in what is disclosed by thought and only by thought, to find a source and standard in reason, cannot be fulfilled through possession of thought as a technique that can be fully mastered. Since then thought, in its process of self-clarification, has differentiated and clarified the methods of cognition and the operations of logic, made them available as it were, and has thus vastly enhanced its own possibilities. But thought still needs its encompassing source, without which it becomes mere logical understanding, a technique, a meaningless bundle of undirected skills. Thought cannot be exhausted by a perfected thinking about thinking.

Hence Socratic thought did not found the sciences; this had been done long before by the Ionian investigators of nature. But from this new thinking the sciences derived an unprecedented impulse.

Nor did Socratic thought inaugurate the philosophical interpretation of the hieroglyphics of being; this had been done in the grand style by the pre-Socratic philosophers. But in Socratic thought this metaphysical thinking was at once transformed and justified. The thinking of the pre-Socratics was naïve, that of the Sophists was "sophisticated." The light with which Socrates illumined them both was the marvelous new naïveté which ever since then has made life possible for the man who is given to himself in self-acceptance. Socrates took over the boundless reflection of the Sophists, but with it he did not seek to dissolve the human substance; rather, he strove to actualize the substance of thought itself and awaken it to inner action.

Every subsequent Socratic thinker has formed his idea of what thought is. But when it comes to the actual practice of thinking, the question is still open. No one has been able to establish theoretically what Socratic thought actually is. But thought it remains. By characterizing Socrates as the inventor of the concept (i.e., the discourse that leads from the particular to the universal), Aristotle, speaking in terms of his own thinking, formulated an idea which had been richly developed by Plato, but which he himself perhaps no longer understood.

Socratic thinking is in danger of taking two false roads, but it can avoid them both. On the one hand, it can degenerate into the morality that offers abstract justification of what it esteems to be correct behavior. On the other hand, it can seek justification in irrationality. In avoiding both errors, it remains oriented toward the germ of unassailable certainty which is actualized in every authentic act of thought.

It is a kind of thinking which does not permit a man to close himself. It will not put up with the evasions of those who refuse to bare their innermost thought; it shakes the complacency of those who trust blindly to fortune, who content themselves with a life of the instincts, or who become too narrowly involved in the interests of personal existence. This kind of thinking opens men's minds and invites the risks of openness.

Where the influence of Socrates is felt, men convince themselves in freedom; they do not subscribe to articles of faith. Here we find friendship in the movement of truth, not sectarianism in dogma. In the clarity of human possibility, Socrates meets the Other as an equal. He wants no disciples. And for this same reason he likes to neutralize his overwhelming personality by speaking ironically of himself.

Socrates - began the philosophy of nonknowledge - question all - remain open - within oneself thru dialogue with others is truth - Perhaps the truth is everything is uncertain -

BUDDHA

There is no certain textual record of Buddha's words. The document containing the oldest accessible traditions is the compendious Pali canon, above all the *Dīgha Nikāya*. The scholars tell us about the available texts, the various trends of the Buddhist tradition in the north and south, and the earliest definitely historical reality: Asoka and his Buddhist teaching two hundred years after Buddha's death. The scholars also show us the great transformations in Buddhism. They try to arrive at the reality of Buddha by a critical excision of obviously legendary material and facts demonstrably of a later period. But there is no conclusive evidence by which to determine how far the excision should go. With these excisions anyone who is looking only for absolute certainties will arrive at a point where nothing is left.

A satisfactory picture of Buddha can only be based on a profound emotion springing from all those passages in the texts which can convincingly (though never with certainty) be traced back to Buddha.

1. LIFE (c. 560–480 B.C.)

Gautama the Buddha was descended from the noble family of the Sakyas who shared in governing the small state of Kapilavastu near the powerful principality of Kosala. He grew up beneath the snowy summits of the Himalayas, which could be seen glittering in the distance throughout the year. As a boy and young man Gautama experienced the worldly happiness of his wealthy aristocratic world. His son Rahula was the fruit of an early marriage.

His happiness was shattered when he became conscious of the basic facts of existence. He saw old age, sickness, death. Horror and disgust at the wretchedness of the flesh are ill becoming to me, he said to himself, for I too shall grow old, sicken, and die. "As I thought these thoughts, all my courage failed me." The consequence was his decision (which took traditional Indian forms) to leave his home, his country, his family, and his wealth, to seek salvation in asceticism. He was twenty-nine years old. One narrative runs: "As a young man in the bloom of his youth, in the first flush of life, the ascetic Gautama left his home and went into homelessness. Though his parents did not wish it, though they shed tears and wept, the ascetic Gautama had his hair and his beard shorn off and put on yellow garments."

Instructed in the ascetic exercises of Yoga, he practiced mortification of the flesh for many years in the woods. "When I saw a cowherd or one who was gathering wood, I fled from forest to forest, from valley to valley, from peak to peak. And why? In order that I should not see them and that they should not see me." For meditation demands solitude. "Verily, this is a lovely bit of earth, a beautiful wood; clear flows the river and there are delightful places in which to bathe; round about there are villages. This is a good place for a noble man striving for salvation." Here sits Gautama, waiting for the moment of Enlightenment, his "tongue cleaving to his palate," "clutching, squeezing, tormenting" his thoughts.

But all in vain. His mortification brings no awakening. He comes to understand that the truth remains veiled in asceticism which is nothing more than asceticism, that empty constraint accomplishes nothing. Then he does something monstrous in the eyes of his Hindu faith; he begins to eat plentifully in order to restore his strength. Regarding him as a renegade, the ascetics with whom he has made friends break with him. He is alone, practicing pure meditation without asceticism.

One night as he meditated beneath a fig tree, the Great Awakening came to him. All at once a vision made everything clear to him: what is; why it is; how beings are caught up in blind lust for life; how they stray from body to body in a never-ending chain of rebirths; what suffering is, whence it comes, how it can be overcome.

His insight is uttered as a doctrine: neither worldly pleasure nor ascetic mortification of the flesh is the right way of life. The former is ignoble, the latter is rich in suffering, and neither leads to the goal. Buddha's discovery is the Middle Path. It is the path of salvation. It starts from the belief, not yet illumined by understanding, that all existence is suffering, and that the essential is redemption from suffering. Then, by way of the decision to live righteously in word and deed, the Path leads to immersion in various degrees of meditation and through meditation to the knowledge of what was already present in the initial faith: the truth of suffering. It is only at the end that one attains clear knowledge of the Path one has traveled, Enlightenment. The circle closes, fulfillment is achieved. This Enlightenment is the step from endless coming-into-being and passing-away to eternity, from worldly existence to Nirvana.

For seven days Gautama, now the Buddha (the Enlightened One), squats at the foot of the fig tree, tasting the joy of redemption. And then what? In the certainty of his Enlightenment, he resolves to keep silent. His knowledge is foreign to the world. How can the world be expected to understand him? Why put himself to "vain trouble"? The world will take its inevitable periodic course through eras of destruction and eras of re-creation; the blind, unknowing creatures will be carried along forever by the wheel of rebirths, in the rise and fall of their forms of existence. The actions performed in any present existence are the *karma* that determines the form of the next rebirth, just as this existence was itself determined by a preceding one. The world does not change, but in it salvation is possible for the Knowing One. Liberated from further rebirths, he enters into Nirvana. Buddha acquired this knowledge in solitude. "No man is my friend." He knows of his redemption. "Enough, I will not reveal it to others; from those who live in love and hate the doctrine remains hidden."

But Buddha cannot persevere in his self-sufficiency, keeping his redemption to himself. After an inner struggle he decides to divulge his doctrine. He does not expect much, and later, when his preaching attracts throngs of people, he predicts that the true doctrine will not long endure. But he continues on his helping way. "In a world grown dark I will beat the deathless drum."

His preaching begins in Benares, where he attracts his first disciples. He was to live for another forty years, wandering, teaching in the vast territories of northeastern India. Spiritually, nothing new happened in him. The core of his sermons was a finished doctrine; he varied an identical theme. Consequently, one can speak of this period only as a whole. Buddha taught in lectures, stories, parables, maxims; we hear of dialogues, of countless scenes and situations, of conversions. He preached not in Sanskrit, but in the vernacular. He thought in concrete images, but he made use of concepts taken over from Hindu philosophy.

His immense historical influence rests very largely on the monastic communities he founded. The disciples left home and occupation and family. They wandered far and wide, in poverty and chastity, tonsured and clad in yellow monks' robes. Having attained the redemption of Enlightenment, they desired nothing more in this world. They lived by begging, carrying bowls into which the people put food as they passed through the villages. From the very start the communities had their rules and regulations, their leaders and discipline. They were joined for periods of time by lay companions, including kings, wealthy merchants, nobles, famous courtesans. All were generous with their gifts. The monastic communities came into possession of parks and houses where large throngs who wished to receive the doctrine could be lodged during the rainy season.

As it spread, this monasticism met with resistance. "The people grew restive: The ascetic Gautama has come to bring childlessness, to bring widowhood, the end of the generations. Many noble youths are turning to the ascetic Gautama to live in holiness." When the throngs of monks appeared, the people mocked them: "Here they come, the baldheads. Here they come, mawkishly hanging their heads in meditativeness; yes indeed, they are as meditative as a cat lying in wait for a mouse." But for Buddha it was a matter of principle to offer no resistance. "I fight not with the world, ye monks. The world fights with me. He who proclaims the truth, ye monks, fights with no one in the world." The struggle was carried on with spiritual weapons. Buddha did not confront a united spiritual power. The Vedic religion had many tendencies; there were already ascetic communities, there were numerous philosophies and even a sophist technique of confusing an adversary with many questions, each of the possible answers to which involved him in contradictions. But since Buddha rejected the sacrifices of the Vedic religion and the authority of the Vedas themselves, his preaching was a radical break with the whole traditional religion.

The texts give us a colorful picture of the life and activity of Buddha and his monks. The rainy season obliged them to spend three months in the house with its vast halls and storerooms, or by the lotus ponds in the adjoining park. The rest of the year was spent in wandering. On their wanderings the monks were lodged by the faithful or slept in the open. When groups of monks met, an immense hubbub arose. When Buddha was about to appear, someone hushed them, for he was a lover of peace and quiet. In carriages or on elephants came kings and merchants and nobles to speak with Buddha and the monks. Each day Buddha himself took up his beggar's bowl and passed from house to house. Throngs of disciples followed him everywhere, and lay companions accompanied the procession, some in wagons bearing provisions.

The memory of Buddha's death and the period preceding it has been preserved. The date of his death, 480 B.C., is regarded as certain. His last wandering is described in detail. At first he tried to get the better of his painful illness and cling to his life. But then he put his will behind him: "Three months hence the Perfect One will enter into Nirvana." Journeying onward, he casts a last glance back at the beloved city of Vesali. As they enter a little wood, he gives his last instructions: "Make me a bed between two twin trees, my head to the north. I am tired, Ananda." And he lay down as a lion lying down to rest.

When one of his disciples wept, he said: "Not so, Ananda. Do not mourn, do not lament. Have I not taught you that it is in the very nature of all things near and dear to us to pass away? How then, Ananda, since whatever is brought into being contains within itself the inherent necessity of dissolution, how can it be that such a being should not be dissolved?"

The disciples believe that with Buddha's death the word will have lost its master. "Think not so. The doctrine and the order that I have taught you, they will be your master when I am gone. The Perfect One thinks not that it is he who should lead the brotherhood. . . . I am now grown old, my journey is drawing to its close, I am turning eighty years of age. Therefore, O Ananda, be ye lamps unto yourselves. Rely on yourselves. Hold fast to the truth as a lamp. Seek salvation alone in the truth."

His last words were: "All accomplishment is transient. Strive unremittingly." Then, rising from one stage of contemplation to the next, Buddha entered into Nirvana.

2. DOCTRINE AND MEDITATION

Buddha's doctrine means redemption by insight. The right knowledge is in itself redemption. But both in origin and method, this redeeming knowledge is very different from our usual conception of knowledge. Buddha's knowledge is not demonstrated by sense perception and logical operations, but springs from experience in the transformations of consciousness and the stages of meditation. Such meditation brought Buddha Enlightenment under the fig tree. The doctrine he handed down could only have sprung from meditation. In meditation Buddha, like all Indian Yogis, knew himself to be in contact with beings and worlds of transcendent origin. In meditation he saw "with the divine, clear-sighted, suprasensory eye."

Science and philosophical speculation remain within our given form of consciousness. But this Indian philosophy may be said to take consciousness itself in hand, to raise it to higher forms by exercises in meditation. Consciousness becomes a variable. Rational thinking confined to space and time—a mere stage of consciousness—is surpassed by the transcending experience of an ascent to the supraconscious.

The answer to the basic questions of existence is to be drawn from these deeper sources, which first lend meaning and justification to the conclusions of reason. Thus what Buddha wishes to reveal is lost in the words that can be said quickly and the abstract propositions that can be thought quickly which make up his teaching. "Deep is the doctrine, hard to behold, hard to understand, full of peace, magnificent, inaccessible to mere reflection, subtle; only the wise man can learn it."

To this way of thinking, the truth both of the philosophical thought that takes place in normal consciousness and of experience in meditation goes hand in hand with a purification of one's whole life by ethical action. Falsehood cannot be overcome by acts of thought alone or by the technique of the transformation of consciousness; these methods can succeed only where the soul has been purified.

What Buddha teaches is not a system of knowledge but a path of salvation, "the Noble Eightfold Path": right views, right aspiration, right speech, right conduct, right means of livelihood, right endeavor, right mindfulness, right meditation. Yet this coherent picture of the path of salvation is itself a form of pedagogic system. Buddha's truth is not based solely on meditation but also takes normal consciousness into account. The understanding is transcended, but not rejected. It is called back into use the moment the experience of transcendence has to be communicated. And it would be equally incorrect to say that Buddha's truth is based entirely on speculative thought, though its forms of expression are drawn from this source. Nor is it subsumed in the ethos of monastic life. Meditation, understanding, philosophical speculation, monastic ethos, all are part of the truth, but each has a kind of independence; they stand in no definite hierarchical order but operate side by side like the different forms of Yoga in all Hindu systems (the training of the bodily energies, the path of ethical works, the rise to enlightenment, immersion in love [*bhakti*], the transformation of consciousness by meditation).

There is no definite relation between the stages of meditation and the ideas accessible to the normal understanding, or between the experience gained by operating with ideas and that gained by operations affecting the state of consciousness. But we find certain parallelisms. In each stage of meditation, for example, a new suprasensory world is experienced. To disregard a reality in order to transcend it is a formal operation that can be performed even without such experience. Logical ideas create space by freeing us from our bonds with the finite. But it is only by meditation that truths are reinforced and established, that full certainty is attained. It cannot be said that the one is primary, the other a mere consequence. One is, rather, the confirmation and guarantee of the other. Each in its own way prepares us for the truth.

In speculation, meditation, and ethos alike, it is the human will that sets the goal and attains it. Each man has his own power of action and conduct, meditation and thought. He works, he struggles, he is like a mountain climber. That is why Buddha is forever calling for an effort of the will. All a man's powers must be engaged. Not all who try achieve the goal. To be sure, there are exceptional cases of spontaneous Enlightenment without effort of the will, especially under the personal guidance of Buddha. Then the goal is attained all at once, and for the remainder of the adept's life it is merely clarified by repetition.

Meditation is not a technique that can succeed by itself. It is dangerous to gain a systematic control over one's states of consciousness, to conjure up one and dispel another. Such methods are ruinous for those who attempt them without the proper foundation. And the foundation is the purity of one's whole life. In the conduct of life the main requirement is "wakefulness," which is carried over into meditation, where it attains its fullest scope. Then awareness permeates the body, illumines the unconscious down to the last nook and cranny. To carry light into the depths is the principle of the ethos, of meditation, and of speculation as well. The stages of meditation should not consist of intoxication, ecstasy, or the enjoyment of strange states such as those induced by hashish and opium, but of insight exceeding all normal insight in brightness, an insight in which the thing is present and one is not merely thinking about it. The universal imperative is thus: let nothing lie dormant in the unconscious, wreaking its havoc; let perfect wakefulness accompany all your action and experience.

Accordingly, the Buddhist monks were enjoined to truthfulness both in their deepest thoughts and in the actions and words of everyday life. They were further enjoined to be chaste, to abstain from intoxicating drink, not to steal, not to harm any living creature (*ahimsa*), and to observe the four modes of inner conduct: loving-kindness, compassion, sympathetic joy, equanimity toward the impure and evil. These four "immeasurables" are raised to infinite heights by meditation. They are the atmosphere of the Buddhist existence: infinite gentleness, nonviolence, the magic that attracts the beasts and appeases their wildness, compassion, friendliness toward everything that lives, whether man, beast, or god.

3. THE EXPRESSED DOCTRINE

In the texts Buddha's doctrine is represented as a body of knowledge, expressed in propositions and rational sequences of ideas accessible to normal consciousness. To be sure, this knowledge has its source in an enhanced state of consciousness, in meditation. But though its certainty springs from an extramundane vision of total self-extinction, the content of this certainty seems to be accessible to the normal understanding. Buddha's lessons communicate not suprasensory experience but a body of rational thought. They disclose a love of concepts, abstractions, enumerations, and combinations, fully consonant with the Indian philosophical tradition on which it draws. But though Buddha's doctrine is accessible to normal consciousness, it cannot be effective without suprasensory experience. The rational thinking of our finite mind is not an adequate vessel for it. The core of the doctrine is perceived only by meditation, and rational formulation can give no more than a pale shadow or intimation of it. The source and context of this doctrine must not be forgotten as we now turn to its simple rational expression.

A. *Buddha's vision of existence is expressed in the truth of pain:* "This is the truth of pain: birth is painful, old age is painful, sickness is painful. . . . Contact with unpleasant things is painful, not getting what one wishes is painful.

"This is the truth of the cause of pain: that craving which leads to rebirth, combined with pleasure and lust, namely the craving for sensual pleasure, the craving for existence, the craving for nonexistence.

"This is the truth of the cessation of pain: the cessation without a remainder of that craving, abandonment, forsaking, release, non-attainment.

"This is the truth of the way that leads to the cessation of pain: it is the Noble Eightfold Path."

This insight springs, not from observation of the particulars of existence, but from a vision of the whole. It reflects not a pessimistic mood, but a serene insight—for in knowledge lies redemption. Serenely Buddha describes the state of existence in ever new variations.

"All things are on fire. The eye is on fire; forms are on fire. . . . And with what are these on fire? With the fire of passion, I say, with the fire of hatred; with birth, old age, death, sorrow, misery, grief and despair are they on fire."

But the heart of the matter is that men, like all living creatures, are blind, unknowing, deluded by the things to which they cling, by what never *is,* but is forever caught up in absolute transience, in coming and going, in never-ending becoming.

Thus there is only one means of liberation: to transcend ignorance by knowledge. But nothing can be changed by insight into particulars here and there. It is only the fundamental state of vision in which we see the whole that transforms and saves. Salvation lies in liberation from attachment to things, in release from all vain craving—these confer insight into the condition and origin of this whole existence and the means of annulling it. Ignorance itself, blindness, attachment to the finite, are the source of this existence; perfect knowledge is its annulment.

B. The coming-into-being of this painful existence through ignorance and its annulment by knowledge are formulated as a "twelvefold concatenation of cause and effect":

"On ignorance depends *karma;* on *karma* depends consciousness; on consciousness depend name and form; on name and form depend the five organs of sense; on the five organs of sense depends contact; on contact depends sensation; on sensation depends desire; on desire depends clutching; on clutching depends existence; on existence depends birth; on birth depend old age and death, sorrow, lamentation, misery, grief and despair."

This chain of causality seems very strange to us. The current interpretation is as follows: it concerns not the cosmic process in general, but only the painful cycle of rebirths (*samsara*): wretched are sickness, old age, and death. What is required to make these possible? Birth. What is the source of birth? Existence . . . and so on down to the first cause, ignorance. If we reverse the order and start from the source, ignorance gives rise to the unconscious powers of formation (*sanskara*), which build the house of life. They carry over from the preceding life and in the present life the first thing they produce is consciousness; through the five senses consciousness sees everything in the name and form of bodily existence. Thence comes contact, then sensation, then desire and physical union—the foundation of future becoming (*karma*), leading once more to birth, old age, and death. This is the doctrine of which it has been said: "The truths that flow from a cause—the Perfect One teaches their cause and how they come to an end." All being is a conditioned becoming.

The knowledge of the chain of causality and of the last cause can dispel this whole nightmare. Once ignorance is overcome, the chain of causality arising from ignorance is also annulled.

In this doctrine the knowledge which is the basis of all salvation is objectivized. It is not a mere knowing about something, but an action and indeed an all-encompassing action. It is identical with the abolition of existence and all its misery. Existence is not abolished by suicide, which merely brings more suffering, other rebirths and other deaths. It ceases only in and with knowledge.

Whence comes the original ignorance from which all the ensuing links of misery follow? The question is not asked. There is no discussion of the primordial fall from eternal perfection into ignorance, an event that might remind one of the Judaeo-Christian fall of man. The series of questions advancing from step to step would seem to imply such an event as the first cause of the world's wretchedness. But here Buddhist questioning stops. Knowledge has provided the certainty of redemption and that is enough. In any case, no guilt is attached to the event with which the misery began; who indeed could be guilty?

c. That is the next question: What is the who? What is the self? Who am I? Buddha's answers are astonishing. *He denies the self.*

The doctrine is formulated as follows: There is no self. Existence is made up of factors which form links in the chain of causality, namely the five senses and their objects (corporeity, sensation, perception); it includes the unconscious formative powers (*sanskara*) which are at work in the predispositions, drives, instincts, the constructive powers of vitality; and finally consciousness. These factors disintegrate in death. Their unity and center is not the self but *karma*, which in rebirth creates another transient combination.

But this formulation veils the meaning which is expressed with the same concepts but more clearly in other contexts, where Buddha does not deny the self, but shows that no thought can penetrate to the true self. "The body is not the self, sensations are not the self, ideas, forms, the unconscious powers of formation, are not the self; cognition, pure intellectual consciousness, is not the self (there is no one invariable self). What is subject to change is not mine, it is not I, it is not my self." But here what is not the self is measured against the standard of a true self. The question of such a self remains open, but a hint is given of the direction in which it is to be sought. Though not explicitly conceived as such, it must coincide with Nirvana.

In lessons derived from the stages of meditation, three stages of the self are expounded: first, the self as *this body;* second, the self as a spiritual body which in meditation is drawn from this body "as a blade of grass from the stalk"; this self belongs to the realm of suprasensory forms; third, the unformed self "consisting of consciousness," which belongs to the infinite realm of the ether. Each self clearly pertains to a stage of meditation, having validity for this stage but no existence of its own. There is no true self. In sensory existence the body is the self. In the first stage of meditation, the spiritual self of the ethereal body becomes real, the former self vanishes into nothingness. But in higher stages the spiritual self is itself annulled. Thus even in meditation the self is not denied, but is shown to be relative. The true self is attained only at the highest stage which coincides with Nirvana.

But if the doctrine cannot, or simply does not, say what the self is, the question arises: Who benefits from redemption? Who is saved? No I, no self, no individual?

D. *What then is?* The stream of becoming which is never being. The illusion of a self which is in truth no self. What is is at once illusion and ignorance and misery. Becoming is a chain of momentary existences, as more fully elaborated by later Buddhism; it is the mere momentariness of the nonbeing of everything that seems to be. There is no permanence, nothing that remains identical. Nowhere is there a fixed point. The self is the illusion of a transient and ever changing something which regards itself as a self.

The stream of becoming and the illusion of selfhood have no foundation in anything else. But both can and should be transcended into something totally different, in the presence of which all forms of thought situated within illusory becoming and selfhood are without validity. Here there is neither being nor nonbeing. This state is revealed to enlightened insight and is attained in Nirvana.

E. *Enlightenment* is the clear-sighted vision attained at the highest stage of meditation. But enlightenment is also the insight which, in the normal state of consciousness, transforms our whole representation of being and the self. This insight sees the world of *samsara,* it sees all the spheres of the world and all the paths of rebirth from the elements to the spheres of the gods and the domains of hell. It sees the cause and the course of suffering and indeed everything which the doctrine communicates inadequately in rational propositions.

F. *Nirvana:* This insight can attain to Nirvana, the ultimate redemption and goal of redemption. How can Buddha speak of Nirvana? When he speaks, he must after all be speaking in the realm of illusory consciousness. When he speaks of Nirvana, it turns into being or nothing. Thus his speaking must assume a special character: it must speak of what to our object-bound opinion is nothing, and yet in so doing say what is all-important. But what is that?

As we have seen, the illusion of becoming and of the self has no ground outside it. There is no escaping into a ground or into another world. But becoming and the self can be wholly transcended into a "realm" where illusion ceases and with it the thinking that we practice in our existence.

We must bear in mind these paradoxes that defy logical understanding if we wish to get at the meaning of what Buddha says about Nirvana. A few examples:

"There exists that condition wherein is neither earth nor water nor fire nor air: where is neither the sphere of infinite space nor of infinite consciousness nor of nothingness nor of neither-consciousness-nor-unconsciousness; where there is neither this world nor a world beyond or both together nor moon-and-sun. Thence is no coming to birth; thither is no going from life; therein is no duration; thence is no falling; there is no arising. It is not something fixed, it moves not on, it is not based on anything. That indeed is the end of ill."

Here inevitably metaphysical forms of thinking set in. Nirvana is said to be absence of duality, neither being nor nonbeing (as in the *Upanishads*), unknowable in the world with the world's methods, hence not an object of investigation, but of the ultimate, most intense certainty. "There is something unborn, which has neither become nor been made nor been formed. If this were not, it would be impossible to find a way out" (as in *Parmenides*). But by the very nature of speech, all speaking of this eternity must miss the mark.

At this point questioning ceases. Those who continue to inquire receive this answer: "You have not known how to observe the limits of questioning. For in Nirvana the holy wandering finds solid ground; Nirvana is its ultimate goal, Nirvana is its conclusion." Those who have not attained to Nirvana can only keep silent and accept their lot. "He who has gone to rest, no measure can measure him. To speak of him there are no words. What thought might comprehend has been annulled: so likewise has every path of discourse been annulled."

G. *Not metaphysics but a way of salvation:* All the ideas of which we have been speaking relate to redemption. Buddha rejects any knowledge that is not necessary to salvation. He declined to explain such propositions as the following: "The world is eternal" and "The world is not eternal," or "The world is finite," "The world is not finite," or "The saint is after death," "The saint is not after death." In other words, he dismissed the questions embodied in such statements.

Buddha even regarded the theoretical treatment of metaphysical questions as harmful. It becomes a new fetter, because metaphysical thinking clings to the very forms of thought, from which a man must free himself if he is to find the way to salvation. Metaphysical speculation results in quarrels and controversies, which lead us to regard our own position as the only true one. But the main reason for declining to answer metaphysical questions is that they do not advance us along the road to Nirvana. They bar the way to redemption:

It is as if a man had been wounded by an arrow thickly smeared with poison, and his friends were to procure for him a physician, and the sick man were to say, "I will not have this arrow taken out until I have learnt the name of the man who wounded me, until I have learnt whether the man who wounded me was from this or that village." That man would die without ever having learnt this. In exactly the same way, anyone who should say, "I will not lead the religious life under the Blessed One until the Blessed One shall explain to me either that the world is eternal or that the world is not eternal," that man would die before the Blessed One had ever explained this to him. Whether the dogma obtain that the world is eternal or that the world is not eternal, there still remain birth, old age, sorrow, lamentation, misery, grief and despair, for the extinction of which in the present life I am prescribing. Accordingly, bear always in mind what it is that I have not explained and why I have not explained it.

His refusal to speak of these things, says Buddha, does not mean that he does not know them. The power of silence that played so large a part in Buddha's life is wonderfully effective in the communication of his thinking. By not touching on all these ultimate things, he leaves them open. His silence concerning them does not spirit them away but leaves them perceptible as a vast background. It is considered possible to find in the world the path by which the world will disappear. The knowledge connected with the traveling of this path is imparted. But we must humbly forgo the knowledge of being as a whole.

4. WHAT IS NEW IN BUDDHA?

There was nothing particularly new in Buddha's doctrines, terminology, forms of thought, conceptions, or actions. Ascetics, ascetic communities, and the practice of monastic life already existed. The forest hermits came of all castes and were looked upon as saints regardless of their origin. The idea of redemption by knowledge was there before him, as was Yoga (the path of the stages of meditation). And Buddha unquestioningly took over old conceptions of the cosmos, the ages of the world, and the world of the gods. The whole Buddhist doctrine may appear to be the perfection of a Hindu form of life grounded in transcendence, a culmination of Hindu philosophy.

The category of the "new" as a standard of value is peculiar to the modern Western world. But even though all the particulars of this great figure's life and thought may be characterized as not new, even so, the category of the new may be applied to certain factors which precisely were responsible for Buddha's vast influence.

A. First of all, Buddha's imposing *personality*. Through the legends we can feel the powerful presence of the historical man. He shows men what they should do. But as for the metaphysical ground of being and ignorance, he leaves it open. It is to this silence that the Sakyamuni (the Silent One from the family of the Sakyas) seems to have owed his compelling influence.

His life was molded by an intense effort of the will. In the legend, the sage Asita predicted that the newborn babe would either be a mighty ruler or a Buddha. But for Buddha the will to conquer and shape the world was not man's full, sovereign will. The sovereign will is found where a man conquers himself, declining to be a prisoner either of himself or of his worldly tasks. "To master the pride of defiant selfhood, that in truth is the highest bliss."

So perfect is his self-conquest that all sign of effort vanishes. Buddha's life of the spirit, released from all bonds, is disclosed by the nobility, serenity, and infinite gentleness of his manner. He never concerns himself with the personal lives and individual secrets of men; they are as far removed from him as the transcended realities of his own life. He has become impersonal; innumerable Buddhas in earlier ages of the world have done what he is doing and will continue to do so in future ones. He vanishes as an individual amid the uncounted multitudes of his peers. "Without house and home, my spirit removed from the world, I walk beyond all ties with men." He is unknowable: "Buddha, he who walks through infinity, leaving no trace: how might you know him?"

The absence of all characteristic features is a part of our picture of Buddha's personality. He is without unique individuality. There are no essential differences between Buddha and his pious disciples or between one and another of the disciples. They are all little Buddhas. Buddha appears as a type, not as a personality. Over against him stand other types, the wicked, the unbelievers, the sophists. Here, paradoxically, is a personality which owes its influence to the extinction of all individual traits. The negation of the self is a basic principle of Buddha's truth. Buddha's fundamental experience cannot have been an experience of historical selfhood, but only of truth in self-extinction. It is the power of the personality without the Western or Chinese consciousness of individuality.

B. Another new feature is that Buddha did *wholly and radically* what before had been done here and there and partly. He turned away from tradition, above all from the caste system and the supreme power of the gods. He did not oppose the gods, he acknowledged them as realities in the workings of the world. But without repudiating them, he reduced them to unimportance.

He was radical in addressing *all men*. What had been possible for a few became possible for everyone. What had happened in small groups of forest hermits was attempted out in the open, in the cities, in the countryside, among men at large, by the monastic communities into which the masses poured. A new existential reality took form: the life of vast throngs of mendicant monks who fulfilled the doctrine by a life of poverty, chastity, homelessness, and unworldliness, while lay companions cared for their material needs.

Actually most of the monks came of the two higher castes. We hear chiefly of "noble youths." Buddha himself was of noble origin. According to later Buddhist doctrine, a Buddha can be born only as a Brahman or noble. Buddhism was an aristocratic religion, and this it remained insofar as only men of a certain intellectual rank can understand it. But the revelation is addressed to all who possess the vocation for it, and in principle to all men; did Buddha not ordain that each man should learn the doctrine in his own language?

Thus for the first time in history the idea of humanity, of a religion for the whole world, became a reality. The barriers of caste, nationality, of all appurtenance to a historically grounded order of society, were breached. What in India had been the carefully guarded secret of a privileged few became a truth to be divulged to all.

If we compare this doctrine with the later world religions of the Stoics, the Christians, Islam, what is characteristic of Buddha is that he cared for not only men but for all living things—the gods and the animals as well—that the salvation he had found was meant for them all.

To speak to all is to speak to each individual. Buddha's decision and the life which followed from it became a model: to depart from the laws of house, family, society. He spoke to everyone who heard him as to one having the power to be equally outside of the world: everything depends on your decision. By his inexorable either-or Buddha seized hold of the whole man.

But the faith required for this path of salvation is a knowledge. Although Buddha rejected traditional speculation as a realm of aimless and ruinous quarreling, he adhered to the principle of Hindu philosophy, namely that salvation itself is a knowledge, that redemption is insight and achieved simultaneously with it.

Buddha spoke to individuals and in small circles. Lessons and conversations prepared the way for the insight that each man must attain by his own action. There are many accounts of how the force of Buddha's words facilitated the task, of how the scales suddenly fell from men's eyes: "It is strange, it is as if one were setting up what was overturned, or revealing what was hidden, or showing the way to someone who was lost, or putting a lamp in the dark—even so has the doctrine been expounded by Gautama in many ways."

c. Because the doctrine is addressed to the individual and to all individuals, because it knows itself to be a light that should reach out into the world and shine everywhere, there is another new factor: the conscious mission. Thus from the very start Buddha founded a monastic community which is two things at once: a path of salvation for the individual and a means of propagating the doctrine by journeyings through the world.

5. INFLUENCE

The spread, transformation, and ramification of Buddhism are one of the great themes in the religious history of Asia. Only once consciously fostered from above, by the initiative of a powerful ruler (Asoka), the vast spread of Buddhism was on the whole a quiet, forceful process.

In the texts we breathe a unique atmosphere, never encountered elsewhere in the world, which was wafted deep into Asia. A new metaphysic and way of life became an element of Chinese and Japanese existence, brought a new gentleness to the peoples of Tibet, Siberia, Mongolia. . . .

But a strange thing happened. In India, which produced Buddhism, it died out. Moved by an overpowering instinct, India remained Hindu, choosing to live in castes, with the old gods, in a philosophically conceived totality, and here Buddhism vanished. Conceived as a religion of humanity, it remained dominant for centuries in large parts of India, and a religion of humanity it remained when it died out without violence in the course of a thousand years. Throughout Asia it was a liberator of hitherto dormant depths in the souls of men, but it was everywhere combated and set aside when national strivings came to the fore (in China and Japan).

In the centuries preceding and following the birth of Christ, Buddhism split into a northern and a southern movement, Mahayana (the Great Vehicle in which to cross the waters of *samsara* to the land of salvation) and Hinayana (the Little Vehicle). Hinayana is purer and closer to the origins; compared to it, Mahayana seems like a fall into the mechanical forms of religion. Yet it is worthy of note that Hinayana, which has endured down to our own day in Ceylon and Indochina, has contributed nothing new. It has done little more than carry the traditional material down through the centuries, whereas Mahayana has entered upon a period of living growth which not only satisfies the religious needs of the masses but has also supplied the basis for a new flowering of sublimated speculative philosophy. With its rigid adherence to a once acquired canon and its emphasis on the perfection of the individual, Hinayana may be regarded as a narrowing. Mahayana, on the other hand, is almost entirely open to new and foreign elements and is resolutely concerned with the redemption not only of the individual, but of all beings. Mahayana has developed certain of Buddha's ideas that were neglected in Hinayana, above all, his decision to bring salvation to all beings, gods and men alike. And here too we find the seeds of the sublime ideas that were to be fully explored only much later, in the Mahayanic sects, by Nagarjuna (c. A.D. 200) and others.

But the most important aspect of Mahayana is that it transformed Buddha's philosophy of salvation into a religion. Let us briefly compare this religion with the movement founded by Buddha himself:

A. *Authority and obedience:* The monastic order fostered a sense of community in all those who, each for himself, sought salvation in insight. But soon the faithful ceased to think on their own responsibility; in practice they lived in obedience to an authority. They "took refuge in Buddha, the doctrine, the congregation."

B. *Disappearance of the faith in one's own powers. Buddha becomes a god:* According to Buddha's teachings, it is not prayer, not grace, and not sacrifice that brings redemption, but only knowledge.

This knowledge lies within the power of the individual. It is won by his own insight, based on the power of his own moral conduct. No god bestows insight, the gods themselves are in need of it. Buddha imparts it. Each man who hears it must make it his own. Hence the last words: Strive unremittingly. In this sense, Buddha's doctrine is philosophy. It lies in man's power to acquire it.

But once this faith in redemption by each man's efforts was shaken, Buddhist thinking was bound to undergo a change. Now the Buddhist cries out for a helping god. But the gods themselves are in need of liberation, hence ultimately powerless. The Buddhist seeks help without abandoning his idea of a man who redeems himself by insight. And he obtains it—when Buddha himself becomes a god. A whole new pantheon comes into being, though its figures are not called gods. Buddha, who wished only to bring a doctrine, becomes a divine figure over all the gods. The belief in Buddha's insight is no longer philosophical faith, but faith in Buddha.

Buddha himself, as his last words show, had no desire to attach his wisdom to his person. But the Buddhists did not preserve the *human* veneration which opens the student to the master's teachings. At an early day the impact of Buddha's personality led to his deification. Even in the ancient texts, the epithets given to Buddha are almost innumerable: the Fully Awakened One, the Perfect One, He Who Is Perfect in Knowledge and Conduct, the Knower of the Worlds, the All-seeing One; he is the Conqueror, the Unconquered, the Incomparable Tamer of the Untamed, the Teacher of Gods and Men, the Peerless One, the Incomparable, the Best of Men.

Soon after his death this honored teacher became the object of a cult. Temples were built around his relics. As early as the third century A.D., we find the belief that he was the incarnation of a divine being (similar to the avatars in the religion of Vishnu), who took this lot upon himself for the salvation of living beings. Every earthly Buddha has his transcendent counterpart which can be seen as such in meditation (*dhyana*) and is called *dhyani-buddha*. The earthly Gautama's *dhyani-buddha* was Amida-Buddha or Amitabha, the ruler of the paradise in the west, of the land of Sukhavati, where he receives the faithful after death. There, reborn in the lotus flowers, they lead a blissful existence, until they are ready for the ultimate step into

Nirvana. These transcendent Buddhas in all their many forms are figures who help the believer and to whom he turns in prayer. They dwell in sensuous paradises which are nearer than the mysterious Nirvana to the mortal soul.

With these changes, the Buddha legend expands into an eventful cosmic history full of magic and splendor. Its protagonists are gods, seers, the devil (Mara), and the demons.

c. In the process of transformation which made Buddhism the Asian religion of humanity, it *assimilated ancient themes from the religious traditions* of many peoples in all stages of cultural development. This process of assimilation was made possible by Buddha's view of the world. His radical freedom from the world resulted in an equally radical tolerance toward the world. For all worldliness rests on the same foundation of ignorance; it is an illusion and a veil that must be dispelled. Indifference toward the intrinsic untruth of the world gives all its variants equal rank as starting points from which to transcend it. Thus Buddhism was able to assimilate all the religions, philosophies, forms of life with which it came into contact. Every idea, every ethos, every faith, even those of the most primitive religions, was a possible preliminary stage, a jumping-off place, indispensable as such, but not a goal.

The echo to Buddha's silence was not only the silence of the sovereign Asian inner life, but also a colorful medley of religious images. In practice, what was to be transcended became the substance of life. Foreign religious forms became garments for Buddhist thinking and soon became Buddhist thinking itself. A striking example is Tibet: even the old methods of magic became Buddhist methods, the monastic community became an organized church with secular rule (presenting so many analogies with the Catholic Church that amazed Christians saw it as a work of the devil, a grotesquely distorted imitation of Christianity).

D. *The role of man:* With these transformations the role of man, as the believer saw it, also underwent a change. All men, all beings, have the prospect of becoming Bodhisattvas, or future Buddhas. If the Bodhisattva does not enter into Nirvana, it is only because he wishes to be born again as a Buddha in order to bring salvation to other men. Each man can aspire to this goal, and on his way he is helped by the grace of those who have already become Bodhisattvas, to whom he prays.

To the mind of the faithful, weariness of life is a sign of negative attachment to existence. Indifference to the world is above hatred or love of the world.

For Buddha the only good thing a man could do was to gain salvation by not grasping, not clinging, not resisting. Thus the building and shaping of the world became meaningless. The world is left as it is. Buddha passes through it with no thought of a reform for all. He teaches men to free themselves from it, not to change it. "As a lovely white lotus blossom is not stained by water, so I am not stained by the world."

But in practice the Buddhists live in the world. Their serene liberation from the world can take two possible forms: among the monks, a slipping into passive indifference, patient suffering, sleep; among the lay Buddhists, a participation in the affairs of the world without being drawn into the world. Living actively in the world, they can attain to Nirvana by "non-attachment." The warrior (the Japanese samurai, for example), the artist, all active men can live in heroic serenity as Buddhists. They act as if they did not act. They are present and not present. Life and death do not touch them. They accept both with indifference.

E. *What remains of the original philosophy?* In magnificent works of art and literature we behold this transformed Buddhism with its elaborately sensuous pantheon interposed between the believer and Nirvana. The question arises: What has all this to do with Buddha? And we answer: In the world of the gods, the innumerable rites and cults, the institutions and sects, and the free monastic communities, a vestige of the philosophical origin remains discernible; something of the spiritual light first embodied in Buddha is reflected even in the most primitive figures of later Buddhism. In all Buddhism there remains a trace of his wonderful self-abandonment, of the life that lets itself be wafted into eternity. There remains the Buddhist love which partakes in the suffering and joy of all living beings and refrains from violence. Despite all the terrible things that have happened in Asia as everywhere else, an aura of gentleness lies over the peoples that have been touched by Buddhism. Buddhism is the one world religion that has known no violence, no persecution of heretics, no inquisitions, no witch trials, no crusades.

True to its origin, Buddhism has never known a cleavage between philosophy and theology, between free reason and religious authority. The question of such a distinction has not been raised. Philosophy itself was a religious activity. And this fundamental principle has remained unchanged: knowledge itself is liberation and redemption.

6. WHAT DO BUDDHA AND BUDDHISM
MEAN TO US?

They are far away from us, and this we must not forget. For Buddha, insight requires: exercises in meditation, a life of indifference toward the world and its tasks. It will not suffice to attempt a scientific experiment and see how much we can accomplish with a few Yoga exercises. Nor will it suffice to develop a mood of indifference to the world and devote ourselves to contemplation. Those who have not tested the progress of which they are capable by years of meditative exercises grounded in the proper faith and way of life, can understand only as much as is communicable in rational thought. In Buddha and Buddhism there flows a source which we Westerners have not tapped, and consequently there is a limit to our understanding. We must first of all acknowledge that Buddhism is far removed from us and renounce all quick, easy ways of coming closer to it. To participate in the essence of Buddha's truth, we should have to cease to be what we are. The difference lies not in rational positions but in the whole view of life and manner of thinking.

But the remoteness of Buddhism need not make us forget that we are all men, all facing the same questions of human existence. In Buddha and Buddhism a great solution was found and put into practice. Our task is to acquaint ourselves with it and as far as possible to understand it.

The question is: To what extent can we understand what we ourselves are not and what we ourselves do not practice? I believe that such an understanding is possible if we avoid excessive haste and supposedly definitive interpretations. In understanding, we keep alive potentialities that are locked deep within ourselves, and by understanding we learn not to take our own objective historicity for the absolute, exclusive truth. To my mind, everything that is said in the Buddhist texts is addressed to a normal waking consciousness and must therefore be largely accessible to rational thought.

The fact that Buddha's life was possible and that Buddhist life has been a reality in various parts of Asia down to our own day—this is a great and important fact. It points to the questionable essence of man. A man is not what he just happens to be; he is open. For him there is no *one* correct solution.

Buddha is the embodiment of a humanity which recognizes no obligations toward the world, but which in the world departs from the world. It does not struggle or resist. Looking upon itself as an existence that has come into being through ignorance, it desires only extinction, but this so radically that it does not even yearn for death, because it has found an abode of eternity beyond life and death.

The serenity of Jesus, with his mystical freedom from the world and nonresistance to evil, seems to present a parallel. But in the West all this remained a beginning, a contributory factor; in Asia it became a whole and hence wholly different.

Buddha Thru meditation comes the knowledge (enlightenment) that frees one from material world... supraconscious thought (no awakening) brings Nirvana) (no way to paraphrase) knowledge is redemption

CONFUCIUS

It may seem impossible to arrive at a reliable picture of the historical Confucius through the layers of tradition that obscure it. Although he himself recorded the traditions and his own thoughts, we do not possess a line which in its present form can definitely be attributed to him. Sinologists differ considerably on important questions of fact: Franke, for example, believes that Confucius cannot have known the *I Ching,* which according to tradition was the object of his studies in the last years of his life. And Forke holds that Lao-tzu, who according to tradition was Confucius' honored master, lived considerably after him. The texts offer plausible arguments on both sides. Nevertheless, though many details remain in doubt, we can obtain a historical picture on the basis of those passages in the copious texts which can most convincingly be attributed to him. Through these texts we discern the remarkable unity of his personality, which in many points contrasts with later Chinese portraits. In the early biography by Ssŭ-ma Ch'ien, written in the first century B.C., and in the *Lun-Yü* (the *Analects*), we find features that cannot have been invented. We can also examine the cultural situation in which he lived and thought, and the adversaries who throw light on him.

I. LIFE (c. 551–479 B.C.)

Confucius was born and died in the state of Lu. He lost his father at the age of three and grew up in straitened circumstances, under his mother's care. As a boy he liked to set up sacrificial vessels and to imitate the gestures of ritual. At the age of nineteen he married, and a son and two daughters were born to him. His relations with his wife and children were without cordiality. He was a large man of great physical strength.

At nineteen he entered the service of a noble family as superintendent of parks and herds. At thirty-two he was engaged in teaching the ancient ritual to a minister's sons. At thirty-three he went to Lo-yang, the imperial capital, to study the customs and traditions of the Chou Empire, which by then had actually split into numerous warring states of various sizes, and whose capital remained solely a religious center. On this occasion he is said to have visited Lao-tzu. When Confucius was thirty-four, the prince of Lu, threatened by powerful rivals among the local nobility, was forced to flee. Confucius accompanied him to a neighboring state. Here he heard music, learned how to play, and became so absorbed that he forgot to eat. Returning to Lu, he devoted the next fifteen years to his studies.

At the age of fifty-one he returned to political life, became minister of justice and finally prime minister of Lu. Thanks to his ability, the prince became increasingly powerful. He overcame the nobles of the region and tore down the fortifications of their cities. The land prospered. Frightened by this rise in the fortunes of Lu, a neighboring prince sent the prince of Lu a present of eighty beautiful girls trained in dancing and music and a troop of fine horses. The prince took so much pleasure in the gift that he neglected his government and ignored the counsels of Confucius. After four years of brilliant activity, Confucius gave up his position and left the country, traveling slowly, with interruptions, always in the hope of being called back.

He wandered about for twelve years, from his fifty-sixth to his sixty-eighth year. He went from state to state in the hope that somewhere he would be enabled to put his political doctrine into practice. In all the years he never lost confidence in his calling as political mentor and orderer of the Empire, though occasionally he cried out: "Let me go home, let me go home." When finally, at the age of sixty-eight, he returned to his native state, he lamented in a poem that after all his wanderings through nine provinces there was still no goal in sight for him: men are without insight, quickly the years pass.

He spent his last years quietly in Lu. He accepted no government position. A profound change is said to have taken place within him. Once a hermit had said of him: "Is that not the man who knows that striving is without hope and yet goes on?" All through the years this had been Confucius' greatness. But now he was old and strove no more. He studied the *I Ching*, or *Book of Changes*, so rich in secrets, and completed his systematic groundwork for a new mode of education by committing traditions to writing and by instructing a group of young men.

One morning Confucius felt the approach of death. He walked about the courtyard, humming the words: "The great mountain must collapse, the mighty beam must break and the wise man wither like a plant." When an alarmed pupil spoke to him, he said: "No wise ruler arises, and no one in the Empire wishes to make me his teacher. The hour of my death has come." He lay down and eight days later he died. He was seventy-three years of age.

2. CONFUCIUS' BASIC IDEA: THE RENEWAL

OF ANTIQUITY

In the troubled times following the disintegration of the Empire, Confucius was one of the many wandering philosophers who aspired to save the country with their counsels. All found the way in knowledge, Confucius in knowledge of antiquity. His fundamental questions were: What is the old? How can we make it our own? How can we make it a reality?

This way of looking at the old was itself something new. Past realities are transformed by present reflection. The translation of tradition into conscious principles gives rise to a new philosophy which identifies itself with the old. The philosopher does not advance his ideas as his own. The Jewish Prophets proclaimed God's revelation, Confucius the voice of antiquity. He who submits to the old is saved from the presumption of basing great demands on his own infinitesimal self. He improves his chances of being believed and followed by those who still live in the substance of their origins. Independent thought, springing from the nothingness of mere reason, is futile: "I have gone without food and sleep in order to think; to no avail: it is better to learn." But learning and thinking go hand in hand. One demands the other. "To learn without thinking is vain."

"I am a traditionalist, not one who creates new things: I am faithful, a lover of the old." The substance and source of our being is to be sought in history. His view of history attaches little importance to the great inventors of wagon, plow, ship. True history begins with the founders of society and government, manners and customs. At the beginning stand the ideal figures, Yao, Shun, Yü: they beheld the eternal archetypes in heaven. For these men Confucius has the highest praise: "Only heaven is great; only Yao was equal to it." These greatest of founders and rulers chose the best of men as their successors. Evil began with the Hsia dynasty when the principle of heredity set in. Inevitably the rulers declined in stature. In the end a tyrant, because he was not a ruler, was overthrown, in accordance with the will of heaven, by a revolution which once again appointed a true ruler, T'ang, founder of the Shang (Yin) dynasty. But since the throne remained hereditary, the same thing happened all over again. The last of the dynasty, again a ruthless tyrant, was overthrown in the twelfth century by the Chou dynasty, which once more renewed the age-old Chinese world. But in Confucius' lifetime the new dynasty had become enfeebled in its turn and the Empire had crumbled into innumerable states. Confucius wished to work for a renewal.

This implies a "critical" view of history; in examining the past, Confucius distinguishes between the good and the bad; he selects facts that are worth remembering as models to be emulated or examples to be avoided. Moreover, he knows that in restoring what was good in the past one should not try to make something outwardly identical. "A man born in our days who returns to the ways of antiquity is a fool and brings misfortune upon himself." What he advocates is not imitation of the past but repetition of the eternally true. The eternal ideas were merely more clearly discernible in antiquity. Now, in his own dark times, he wishes to restore them to their old radiance by fulfilling himself through them.

But this belief in a final, eternal truth derives movement from the way in which we assimilate the old. It does not bar our way but spurs us forward. Confucius finds a living solution to the problem of *authority,* which for him is not merely a monopoly on the exercise of violence. Here for the first time in history a great philosopher shows how the new, merging with the tradition flowing from the source of eternal truth, becomes the substance of our existence. He points the way to a conservative form of life, made dynamic by a liberal open-mindedness.

If the truth has been manifested in the past, we shall find it by investigating the past, but in so doing we must distinguish between what was true and what was false. This is done by learning, which means not merely to acquire information about something but to make it our own. This true "learning" is gained by books and schooling. Confucius provided the books by selecting ancient texts, documents, songs, oracles, codes of manners and customs, and reworking them with a view to truth and effectiveness. He laid the groundwork of school education, first of all with his own private school in which he strove to shape young men into future statesmen. With him the *mode of learning* and teaching becomes a fundamental problem. The aim of all learning is *practical efficacy.* "If a man can recite all three hundred pieces in the *Book of Odes* by heart and, entrusted with the government, is unable to perform (his duties) or if, sent abroad as an ambassador, he is incapable of replying on his own, where is the good of all his learning?"

But without learning, all other virtues are obscured as though by a fog and degenerate: without learning, frankness becomes vulgarity; bravery, disobedience; firmness, eccentricity; humanity, stupidity; wisdom, flightiness; sincerity, a plague.

Now let us see how, in the philosophy of Confucius, the new expressed itself in the form of the old. First we shall take up the moral and political ethos culminating in the ideal of the "superior man"; secondly, the ideas constituting the fundamental wisdom; and thirdly, we shall see how an element of uncertainty is introduced into the perfection of this edifice of thought by Confucius' awareness of limits—the limits of education, communicability, knowledge—by his awareness of his own failure and his contact with the factor which sustains his whole work, but at the same time opens it to question.

3. THE MORAL-POLITICAL ETHOS

Manners and music are fundamental. The essential is to shape men's nature, not to quench it. The ethos is fashioned in men's association with each other and in government. It is made manifest in the ideal of the "superior man."

A. *Li:* Order is preserved by customs (*li,* imperatives of conduct). "A nation can be guided only by custom, not by knowledge." The customs create the spirit of the whole and in turn draw their life from it. Only through the virtues of the community does the individual become a man. The *li* are the unceasing education of all men. They are the forms which create the right frame of mind in all spheres of existence: earnestness, confidence, respect. They guide men through something universal which is acquired by education and becomes second nature, so that the individual comes to experience the universal not as a constraint but as his own being. The forms give the individual firmness, assurance, and freedom.

Confucius set forth the *li* as a whole; he observed them, collected them, formulated and arranged them. His vision embraced the whole world of Chinese customs: the right way of walking, greeting, behaving in company, always in accordance with the particular situation; the ways of conducting sacrifices and observing holidays; the rites of marriage, birth, death, and burial; the rules of administration; the customs governing work, war, the family, the priesthood, the court; the order of the days and seasons, the stages of life.

In Confucius there is nothing absolute about the *li.* "A man is awakened by the Odes, strengthened by the *li,* perfected by music." Mere form, like mere knowledge, has no value without the originality that fulfills it, without the humanity that is enacted in it. "A man who does not love his fellow man—what will the *li* avail him?"

He who "overcomes his self and takes upon himself the restrictions of the *li,* the laws of custom"—he becomes a man. Although righteousness is essential, "in practicing it the superior man is guided by the *li.*" There must be a balance between the *li* and the content (a man's original nature). "He in whom the content predominates is uncouth; he in whom the form predominates is a scribe [intellectual dandy]." In the practice of the forms, the essential is "freedom and lightness," but the freedom must be "regulated by the rhythm of set rules." Tzu-Kung wished to do away with the sacrifice that was customary on the first of the month. Said the master: "My dear Tzu, you are concerned with the sheep, I with the custom [*li*]."

Confucius drew no distinction between custom, morality, and justice and thus perceived their common root all the more clearly. Nor did he distinguish between ethical obligation and aesthetic considerations involving no responsibility, between the good and the beautiful. The beautiful is not beautiful unless it is good, while the good to be good must be beautiful.

B. *Music:* For Confucius music, side by side with the *li,* was a primary factor in education. The spirit of the community is formed by the music it hears; in music the individual finds the themes that order his life. Hence the government must encourage one kind of music and forbid another: "Take Shao music with its rhythms, but forbid Chêng music, for the songs of the Chêng are dissolute."

C. *Nature and formation:* Confucius assents to all that is natural. To each thing he assigns its order, its measure, its place, and rejects nothing. He advocates self-mastery, not asceticism. Nature requires to be shaped, but violence can only harm it. Even hatred and anger have their place. The good man can love and hate in the right way. For example: "He hates those who themselves are base and slander those who are above them; he hates the bold who know no morality; he hates the reckless, bigoted fanatics."

D. *Human intercourse:* For Confucius human intercourse is the life element. "The superior man does not neglect his neighbors." But in our association with men, we encounter both good and bad. "Have no friend who is not your equal," says Confucius, but he rejects the maxim: "Associate with those who are worthy of it; as for those who are unworthy, keep them at a distance." Instead he declares: "The superior man honors the worthy and tolerates all men." But in his dealings with others the superior man keeps his wits about him: "He may let others lie to him but not make a fool of him. The superior man encourages what is beautiful in men; the inferior man, what is unbeautiful." Thus the spirit of men living together develops in one direction or the other. "What makes a place beautiful is the humanity that dwells there. He who is able to choose and does not settle among humane people is not wise."

Human relations are governed by the following fundamental attitudes. *Toward the ages of life:* "Let me respect the tranquillity of the ages; let me be loyal to my friends; let me love children tenderly." *The right conduct toward parents:* Serve them in life, bury them properly after death, thereafter sacrifice to them. It is not enough to feed your parents; "if respect is absent, wherein should we differ from the beasts?" In case they seem to be mistaken, we may remonstrate, but respectfully, and we must obey them. A son must cover up his father's mistakes. *Toward friends:* Take no friends who are not at least as good as yourself. Loyalty is the foundation. Friends should "loyally admonish one another and tactfully set one another right." Friends can be relied on: "Even if the season be cold, we know that pines and cypresses are evergreen." *Toward the authorities:* "A good official serves his prince in the right way; if that is impossible, he withdraws." He will "not circumvent the prince but oppose him openly"; "he will not be chary of good advice." "If the country is on the right path, he may speak and act boldly; if it is not on the right path, he may act boldly, but he will speak cautiously." *Toward subordinates:* The superior man gives his servants no ground for complaint that he makes insufficient use of them, but (unlike the inferior man) he does not expect perfection; he takes men's abilities into account and does not dismiss old and trusted servants without grave cause.

One is struck by Confucius' indifference toward women. He has nothing to say of conduct in matrimony, speaks disparagingly of women, has only contempt for a pair of lovers who have committed suicide together, and frequently remarks that nothing is so hard to handle as a woman. The atmosphere around him is distinctly masculine.

E. *Government:* Government is the center of men's lives and all other considerations derive from it. Confucius sees a polarity between what must be made and what must grow. Good government is possible only in a sound social condition, molded by the *li,* the right music, the right modes of human intercourse. Such a condition can only grow. But though it cannot be made, it can be fostered or impeded.

Laws are a means of government. But only to a limited degree do they bring results. And intrinsically, they are harmful. Example is better than law. For where the laws govern, the people are shameless in evading punishment. But where example governs, the people have a sense of shame and improve. When an appeal is made to the laws, it means that something is not in order. "When it comes to hearing complaints, I am no better than anyone else. What interests me is to see that no complaints arise."

A good government must be concerned with three things: sufficient food, a sufficient army, and the confidence of the people. If one of these must be sacrificed, the government can most readily do without the army; next in line comes food ("men have always had to die"); but a government cannot do without confidence. "If the people have no confidence, all government is impossible." But in planning its policy, a government cannot begin with the demand for confidence. Confidence cannot be demanded but must be brought to grow spontaneously. As to policy, above all "make the people prosperous." The next most important thing is to "educate them."

Good government requires a *good prince*. He taps the natural sources of wealth. He chooses carefully what work the people should undertake; then they do not grumble. He is superior without being haughty; whether dealing with many or few, with great or small, he is not disdainful. He commands respect without a show of force. Like the polestar, he stands fast and lets everything move around him in its order. Because he desires the good, the people become good. "If the authorities love good conduct, the people will be easy to handle." "If a ruler is right in his own person, he has no need to command, things are done without commanding."

A good prince knows how to choose the right officials. One who knows and desires the good cannot rule with evil helpers: "Oh, the rabble. Is it possible to serve the prince in collaboration with them?"

Confucius has innumerable maxims about government. All are of a general ethical nature. For example: "Do nothing overhastily; that will not succeed. Do not consider the small advantage, for no great work can prosper in this way." In all these reflections he has in mind a statesman selected by the prince and governing with his consent and understanding. A great statesman proves himself by restoring and reinforcing the ethical-political edifice as a whole.

Such intervention in historical reality is subject to two main principles. (1) A capable man must stand in the right place. "If a man possesses the throne but lacks the necessary strength of mind, he should not venture to make cultural changes. Similarly, if he has strength of mind but not the highest authority, he should not venture to make cultural changes." (2) The political conditions must be such as to make effective action possible. Where the prevailing state of mind leaves no room for effective action, the true statesman remains in hiding. He waits. He refuses to compound with evil, to enter into relations with base people. These principles contain an element of Plato's belief that human conditions will not improve until philosophers become kings or kings philosophers. Confucius spent his whole life looking for a prince to whom he might lend his intelligence. But in vain.

F. *The superior man:* All goodness, truth, beauty are combined in the ideal of the superior man (Chün-tzǔ). Noble both in birth and endowment, he has the manners of a gentleman and the wisdom of a sage.

The superior man is no saint. The saint is born; he is what he is; the superior man becomes what he is through self-discipline. "To have the truth is the path of heaven, to seek the truth is the path of men. He who has the truth finds the right action without pains, achieves success without reflection." But he who *seeks* the truth chooses the good and holds it fast. He investigates, he questions critically, he ponders the truth and resolutely acts on it. "Perhaps others can do it the first time; I must do it ten times; perhaps others can do it the tenth time; I must do it a thousand times. But he who really has the perseverance to go this way—be he foolish, he will become clearheaded; be he weak, he will become strong."

The character, cast of thought, gestures of the superior man are described. He is contrasted with the inferior man. The superior man is concerned with justice, the inferior man with profit. The superior man is quiet and serene, the inferior man is always full of anxiety. The superior man is congenial though never stooping to vulgarity; the inferior man is vulgar without being congenial. The superior man is dignified without arrogance; the inferior man is arrogant without dignity. The superior man is steadfast in distress; the inferior man in distress loses all control of himself. The superior man goes searching in himself; the inferior man goes searching in others. The superior man strives upward; the inferior man strives downward. The superior man is independent. He can endure long misfortune as well as long prosperity, and he lives free from fear. He suffers from his own in-ability, not from others' failure to understand him. He avoids all competi-tion, but if it must be, then only in archery. He is slow in words and quick in action. He is careful not to let his words outshine his deeds: first act, then speak accordingly.

The superior man does not waste himself on what is distant, on what is absent. He stands in the here and now, in the real situation. "The superior man's path is like a long journey; you must begin from right here." "The superior man's path begins with the concerns of the common man and woman, but it reaches into the distance, penetrating heaven and earth."

4. THE BASIC WISDOM

So far we have gathered maxims relating to the political ethos. But through these maxims run certain basic ideas that form a kind of conceptual system.

A. *The great alternative:* Confucius is conscious of facing a great alternative: to retire into solitude or to live in the world and try to shape it. His de-cision is unequivocal: "A man cannot live with the birds and beasts. If I do not live with men, with whom shall I live?" And "he who is concerned only with the purity of his own life ruins the great human relations." In evil times it may seem as though nothing else remains but to go into seclusion and attend to one's own personal salvation. Of two hermits Con-fucius says: "In their private lives they found purity; in their retirement they found what the circumstances demanded. I am different. For me there is nothing that is possible or impossible under all circumstances." His toler-ance toward the hermits only makes him more resolute in regard to his own conduct. "If the world were in order, there would be no need of me to change it."

In this devotion to man and his world, Confucius develops certain ideas that may be stressed as his *basic wisdom*. They relate to the nature of man, to the necessity of a social order, to the question of truth in language, to the nature of our thinking, to the absolute character of the source and the rela-tivity of the manifestation—and finally to the One which holds all things together and to which all things relate. In every case, Confucius' main con-cern is man and human society.

B. *The nature of man:* The nature of man is called *jên*. *Jên* is humanity and morality in one. The ideogram means "man" and "two," that is to say: to be human means to be in communication. The question of the nature of man is answered, first in the elucidation of what he is and should be; second in an account of the diversity of his existence.

First: A man must become a man. For man is not like the animals which are as they are, whose instincts govern their existence without conscious thought; he is a task to himself. Men actively shape their life together and, transcending all instinct, build it on their human obligation.

Humanity underlies every particular good. Only he who is in *jên* can truly love and hate. *Jên* is all-embracing, not a virtue among others, but the soul of all virtues. It is described through its particular manifestations: piety, wisdom and learning, righteousness. Confucius does not derive one virtue from another. *Jên* is the all-embracing source. It is through *jên* that the particular virtue becomes truth. And *jên* is the source of the absolute untainted with expedience: "The ethical man puts the difficulty first and the reward last."

To act according to *jên* is to follow not a definite law but what gives all definite laws their value and at the same time deprives them of any absolute character. Although indefinable, the nature of *jên* is adumbrated: it resides in what Confucius calls measure and mean. "Measure and mean are the summit of human nature." They operate from the inside out: "The state in which hope and anger, grief and joy, are not yet active is called the mean. The state in which they express themselves but always find the right rhythm is called measure." Because the innermost is revealed and everything is decided here at the source, the greatest attention must be devoted to measure and mean: "Nothing is more obvious than what is secret, nothing more evident than what is most hidden; therefore the superior man is attentive to what he is for himself alone."

The notion is mysterious; Confucius adumbrates it with references to the mean between two extremes. "To be magnanimous and mild in teaching and not to punish those who behave badly: that is the strength of the south. To sleep and die in the stable without having to: that is the strength of the north. But the superior man stands in the middle and bends to neither side." Or: "A man may put an empire in order, he may forgo office and honors, he may tread on bare knives—and yet not master the measure and mean."

Second: The nature of man is manifested in the diversity of human existence. Men resemble one another in essence—in *jên*. But they differ "in habits," individual character, age, stage of development, and knowledge.

The ages of life: "In youth when the vital forces are not yet developed, guard against sensuality; in manhood, when the vital forces have attained their full strength, against quarrelsomeness; in old age, when the forces are on the wane, against avarice."

Human types: Confucius distinguishes four types or levels of man. The highest embraces the saints, those who possess knowledge from birth. Confucius never saw a saint but he has no doubt that they existed in antiquity. The second level comprises those who must acquire knowledge by learning; they can become "superior men." The men of the third level find it hard to learn, but they do not let this discourage them. Those of the fourth level find it hard and make no effort. The two middle types are on the way; they progress though they may fail. "Only the highest wise men and the lowest fools are unchangeable."

c. *The source is absolute, the manifestation relative:* Truth and reality are one. The mere idea is as nothing. The root of human salvation lies in the "knowledge that influences reality," that is, in the truth of ideas that are translated into an inner, transforming action. What is true within takes form without.

"Things have roots and ramifications." The absoluteness of the origin enters into the relativity of the manifestations. If the root is good, if it is knowledge, reality, then the ideas become true, consciousness becomes right, the man is cultivated, and further, the house will be well regulated, the state in order, the world at peace. From the Son of Heaven to the common man, education is the root. He who cannot teach the members of his household cannot teach other men. But if "humanity reigns in the house of the serious man, humanity will flower in the whole state."

Because the norms and impulses come from the root or source, from something so deep and wide as to defy definitive formulation, the rules by which we reckon what should be done can never suffice. Truth and reality can never be embodied once and for all in any unchanging state or dogmatic statements. Confucius "had no opinions, no bias, no obstinacy." "The superior man is not absolutely for or against anything in the world. He supports only what is right." He is "not partisan but for all." He preserves his openness. "When he does not understand something, he is reticent." He is "firm in character, but not obstinate," "congenial without stooping to vulgarity," "self-confident but not self-righteous." The absolute appears in the relative. Confucius regards all calculable things as relative—this does not mean that they cease to exist, but that they are guided by a higher principle.

D. *The necessity of order:* Order is necessary because it is only in human association that the essence of man is real. Order is based on a *first principle* which throughout life can serve as a guide to action. "Do to no one what you would not wish others to do to you." In acting on this rule, men are bound by a sense of equality (*shu*). "Do not display to your inferiors what you hate in your superiors. Do not offer your neighbors on the left what you hate in your neighbors on the right."

Among the Confucians we find a positive formulation corresponding to this negative injunction: "The lover of mankind strengthens men, for he himself wishes to be strengthened; he helps men toward success, for he himself wishes to achieve success."

But when Lao-tzu taught that one should repay hostility with good deeds, Confucius answered: "With what then shall we reward good deeds? No, reward hostility with justice, and good deeds with good deeds."

A *second principle* of order is this: Because men are so different, good government is made possible only by degrees of power. The higher the power, the more exemplary, knowing, human, must be he who possesses it. He must "march in advance of the people and encourage them. He must not weary."

Those who are capable of self-mastery, who have learned to do what is good and to know what they are doing, will always be few. The people, on the other hand, "can be led to follow something; they cannot be led to understand it." The fundamental relation of the exemplary man to the people is this: "The essence of the prince is the wind, the essence of the crowd is the grass. If the wind blows over it, the grass must incline." Order is possible only through authority.

Everything depends on the coincidence of official position and human worth. Hence the order must not be reversed. "One who holds no office should not concern himself with government projects." It is necessary "to exalt the good, to abase the wicked, to instruct the awkward."

Thus the man capable of governing is independent of public opinion. "Where all hate, he must examine; where all love, he must examine." When asked, "What kind of man is it that his compatriots love?" Confucius replied: "That in itself means nothing." And when asked, "What kind of man is it that his compatriots hate?" he replied again: "That in itself means nothing. It is better to be beloved of the good among one's compatriots, and hated by those who are not good."

A *third principle* of order is: Once a development has begun, direct intervention can no longer be fruitful. It comes too late. Of course force, laws, punishments can be brought to bear, but the result will be disastrous, for those threatened with violence will evade it and hypocrisy will become universal. Great effects can be achieved only indirectly. What is present in the germ can be guided in a different direction or encouraged. Here decisive action is possible. The human sources must be made to flow; it is from them that everything else follows.

E. *Words must be set aright:* When asked, "What is the first thing to be done in order to promote a renewal in disastrous circumstances?" Confucius gave a remarkable answer: Words must be set aright. What inheres in words should be brought out. The prince should be a prince, the father a father, the man a man. But language is constantly misused, words are employed for meanings that do not befit them. A separation arises between being and language. "He who has the inner being also has the words; he who has words does not always have the inner being."

If the language is in disorder, everything goes wrong. "If words (designations, concepts) are not right, judgments are not clear; works do not prosper; punishments do not strike the right man, and the people do not know where to set hand and foot.

"Therefore the superior man chooses words that can be employed without doubt, and forms judgments that can be converted into actions without fear of doubt. The superior man tolerates no imprecision in his speech."

F. *The one thing on which everything depends:* When men speak of many things, of many virtues, of all that has to be learned and done, Confucius says: "You think I have learned much and know much? No, I have one thing by which to penetrate all." Thus he speaks not of many things, but of one thing. What is it? Confucius has no one unchanging answer. He looks to the one, he speaks of one thing on which everything depends, but when he replies, he refers to one or another of the concepts we have already encountered: *chung* (the mean) or perhaps the one word *shu* (equality, reciprocity, charity). Or he may merely sum up the doctrine: "No one can be regarded as a superior man who does not know the calling of heaven; no one can be regarded as mature who does not know the laws of conduct (*li*); no one can know men who does not understand their words." Or, morality is the love of mankind; wisdom is the knowledge of men. But in all this we have lost sight of the One.

The One becomes more readily discernible in Confucius where a background, a supreme authority, makes itself felt. In developing an idea related to Lao-tzu's *wu-wei* (nonaction), he may find his supreme authority in a saintly ruler of the past (but, he says, such rulers exist no longer): "One who kept the empire in order without doing anything was Shun. For what in truth did he do? He respectfully watched over himself and solemnly turned his face to southward. Nothing more." Apart from this, the One is discernible in Confucius' awareness of limits.

5. CONFUCIUS' AWARENESS OF LIMITS

Thus far we seem to have described the philosophy of Confucius as a knowledge that regards itself as complete and an underlying feeling that everything can and will be set aright. Such a picture of Confucius would be inaccurate.

A. Confucius never thought himself in possession of complete knowledge and never thought such knowledge possible. "To represent what you know as knowledge and what you do not know as ignorance: that is knowledge."

B. Confucius is aware of the evil in the world. It is rooted in the failure of man. He laments: "That good predispositions are not cultivated, that what men have learned is not effectual, that men know their duty and are not drawn to it, that men have faults and are unable to correct them: these are things that grieve me." Sometimes he says he can no longer find a single true man. "It is all over. I have met none able to see his own faults, to look within and accuse himself." Nowhere does he find reliance on the love of humanity and on horror of the inhuman. "I have seen none who loved moral worth as he loves women's beauty." When he looks around for a man who might be a ruler, he finds none. He sees no saint; even to see a superior man would be gratifying, but again there is none; there is not even a persevering man.

Yet Confucius is far from regarding the world as evil. Only the times have degenerated, as had often happened before. Accordingly: "He knows that the truth will not shine through in our day."

c. The last things are never his main theme. He becomes diffident at the approach of the ultimate and seldom speaks of happiness, fate, pure virtue. When asked about death, nature, and the world order, he gave answers that left the question open—not because he was given to secretiveness ("There is no thing that I would withhold from you"), but because the matter itself imposed such answers. Often men are led to the ultimate questions by false motives (curiosity, desire to circumvent present necessities, to evade the road into life). Not only had Confucius no desire to satisfy such motives; still more important was the impossibility of discoursing objectively about what can never, properly speaking, become an object. This is why Confucius refrains from all direct statement on metaphysical questions. Though such an attitude may be put down as agnosticism, it does not signify indifference to the unknowable, but rather a reverence which is unwilling to transform intimation into pseudo knowledge or lose it in words. In Confucius, at all events, the impulse toward the boundless and unknowable, the consuming question of the great metaphysicians, is scarcely discernible; but we do discern the presence of the last things in his pious observance of customs and in maxims which, without explicitly saying much, suggest a way in critical situations.

Confucius shared in the traditional religious conceptions. He did not doubt the existence of spirits and omens. Ancestor cult and sacrifice were for him an essential reality. But in all his dealing with these matters he showed a remarkable aloofness and freedom from superstition. "The master never spoke of magic powers and unnatural demons." "To serve spirits other than one's own ancestors is adulation." Asked about the cult of spirits, he replied: "If you cannot serve men, how shall you serve spirits?" Questioned about wisdom, he answered: "To devote yourself to your duty toward men, to honor the demons and gods and keep away from them, that may be called wisdom." These words are ambiguous. Should one keep a respectful distance from the gods or ignore them as much as possible? But there is no doubt about his earnest observance of the cult: The sacrifice has great meaning but I know not what it is. "One who knew the meaning of the great sacrifice (for the ancestor of the dynasty) would be able to rule the world as easily as to look over here"—and he pointed to the palm of his hand.

Confucius speaks of heaven. "Only heaven is great." "The seasons go their course and all things come into being. But does heaven speak?" Wealth and prestige rest with heaven. Heaven can destroy. This heaven is impersonal. Its name is *tien*; only once is it referred to as *shang-ti* (Lord). Impersonal is the fate that it sends, the will of heaven (*ming* or *tien-ming*). "That is the will of heaven," is one of his frequent locutions.

Confucius seldom speaks of prayer. Suppliant prayer, not to mention magic prayer, is far from him, for he implies (if Wilhelm's translation is accurate) that his whole life is prayer. The words of a Japanese Confucian in the ninth century are quite in the spirit of Confucius: "If only the heart follows the path of truth, you need not pray, the gods will protect you."

"Death and life are the will of heaven"; "From the beginning all men have had to die." Such maxims express Confucius' candid acceptance of death. Death offers no ground for emotion, it is not situated in any field of essential meaning. He can indeed lament premature death: "That some things germinate but do not flower; that some things flower that do not mature—alas, that happens." But: "To die at nightfall, that is not bad." Death has no terrors: "When a bird is dying, his song is mournful; when a man is dying, his speech is good." It is meaningless to inquire about death: "If you do not know life, how should you know death?"

But when asked whether the dead know of the offerings sacrificed to them, he replies: "Knowledge of this is no concern of ours." He judges the answers pragmatically, by their results, and concludes that no answer is the best: "If I say yes, I must fear that pious sons may spend their substance for the departed—if I say no, I must fear that impious sons may neglect their duty toward the departed."

6. THE PERSONALITY OF CONFUCIUS

We have statements that Confucius made about himself, and others that his disciples attributed to their master.

He was *conscious of his vocation*. In a situation of mortal peril, he said: "Since King Wen is no more, has culture been entrusted to me? If heaven had wished to destroy this culture, a latecomer could not have received it. But if heaven does not wish to destroy this culture, what can the men of K'uang do against me?"

Despite his consciousness of his mission, he was a modest man. No doubt, he believed, he could compete with others in learning, but he recognized that he had not attained the level of the superior man who can transform his knowledge into action. "Of myself I can only say that I have striven insatiably to become so, and that I teach others untiringly."

His disciples often criticize him. He justifies his visit to the Lady Nantzŭ: "If I have done wrong, heaven drove me to it." He justifies a breach of oath on the ground that the oath was forced from him by a threat.

When a disciple describes the master's dejection in rather drastic terms, Confucius replies approvingly: "Like a dog in the house of mourning, you've hit it, you've hit it." To a disciple whom a prince has questioned about him, Confucius says: "Why did you not answer thus: He is a man who learns the truth without tiring, who instructs men indefatigably, who is so zealous that he forgets to eat, who is so serene that he forgets all cares, and consequently does not notice the gradual approach of old age."

Confucius sees his own failure. In a situation of dire peril, he asks his pupils: "Is my life wrong? Why does such distress come upon us?" The first says that men do not trust him because he has not yet attained true goodness, nor do what he says because he has not attained true wisdom. But Confucius replies: Saints and wise men of the past have met with the most terrible ends. Clearly goodness is not necessarily rewarded with confidence, nor wisdom with obedience. The second says the master's doctrine is so great that no one on earth can endure it. The doctrine must be reduced a little in stature. In reply to this, Confucius says: The good husbandman can sow but not bring forth the harvest. The superior man can fashion his doctrine but not cause it to be accepted. To concern oneself with its acceptance is not to look into the distance. The third says: "Your doctrine is very great, therefore the world cannot grasp it. But continue to act in accordance with it. What matter that it is not accepted? In that he is not understood, thereby the superior man is known." Confucius smiled.

Confucius did not always calmly accept his failure, but scrutinized and interpreted it. His attitude was not determined in advance and was not always the same.

He could lament: "The superior man suffers that he must leave the world and that his name is not mentioned. My way is not followed. Whereby shall I be known to posterity?" "Ah, no one knows me!" But he quickly consoles himself: "I do not grumble against heaven, I am not angry with men. I have searched here below and I am in communication with heaven. Heaven knows me."

He contents himself with his lot: "To learn and unceasingly practice, does that not give satisfaction? And if companions come to you from far away, is not that too a ground for rejoicing? And not to grow embittered if men do not know you, is not that too noble?" "I will not grieve that men do not know me; I should grieve only if I did not know the others."

The fool calls out to him: "Give up your vain striving. He who wishes to serve the state today only flings himself into peril." And Lao-tzu says to him: "The shrewd and clever are close to death, for they love to judge other men." But he persists in his task of helping to build a human order in the world. Success is not decisive. To be humane means to bear your part of responsibility for the state of the community. "A man of humanity does not strive for life at the cost of injuring humanity. No, there have been men who, to perfect their humanity, have given their body to death."

His basic attitude is one of readiness. "If they use you, be active; if they turn their backs on you, remain in retirement."

But here is the essential: "The one thing over which a man is master is his own heart. Good or ill fortune is no yardstick of a man's value." Not always is outward misfortune an evil; it can be "a test" (Hsün Tzǔ). Despair must not be radical. Even in extreme affliction hope remains. "There are cases in which men rise from desperate circumstances to the highest calling."

Confucius did not exert the influence he had expected in his moments of highest hope. Even after his death his action as he intended it failed as it had failed in his lifetime. For it was only in a modified form that his work became effective. This makes it all the more important to find the original substance which beneath all the modifications was never wholly lost, and to preserve it as a standard. By selecting the most meaningful and characteristic of the available sayings, we may venture to look for a faithful picture. But the picture vanishes if we stress the banal, dogmatic formulations which probably stem from a later day. And the picture resulting from a careful choice and arrangement of Confucius' sayings and the stories about him must have a core of truth, for otherwise it could not have come into being.

Confucius did not turn away from the world to concentrate on himself. He devised no economic institutions, no legislation, no special form of government; he was passionately concerned with something that cannot be directly willed but only fostered indirectly, something on which everything else depends: the spirit of the whole in the ethical-political state and the inner make-up of every individual man as a part of the whole. He had no fundamental religious experience, no revelation; he achieved no inner rebirth, he was not a mystic. But neither was he a rationalist; in his thinking, rather, he was guided by the idea of an encompassing community, through which man becomes man. His passion was for beauty, order, truthfulness, and happiness in the world. And all these are grounded in something that is not made meaningless by failure and death.

Confucius restricted his thinking to possibilities in the world, and this is the source of his moderation. He was cautious and reserved, yet not from fear, but from a sense of responsibility. As far as possible he sought to avoid the doubtful and dangerous. Desiring knowledge, he listened in every quarter. He had an insatiable thirst for knowledge of antiquity. In his sayings, prohibitions are far less frequent than advice to do this and that if you wish to be a man. Observe moderation; keep in readiness. What moves him is no urge for power as such, but the will to true mastery.

His nature strikes us as smiling, open, natural. He rejects all deification of his person. He lives in the street, as it were, a man with his weakness.

What did Confucius do? Unlike Lao-tzu, he entered into the business of the world, driven by the idea that he was called to improve human conditions. He founded a school for future statesmen. He edited the classics. But still more significant: In China, Confucius was the first great flaring up of reason in all its breadth and potentiality—and this in a man of the people.

7. CONFUCIUS AND HIS ADVERSARIES

Confucius combated and was combated. First came the surface struggles against incompetence and the jealousy of his competitors. But there followed the profound, essential polarity between him and Lao-tzu.

A. The adversaries whom Confucius combated were the men who regarded the world as corrupt to begin with and adroitly played their hand in this corrupt world, the sophists who found arguments for or against any cause, who muddled the standards of right and wrong, true and false.

Once when Confucius was in office, he had an aristocrat executed as dangerous to the state. He justified his action: Worse than theft and robbery are: insubordination combined with guile, mendacity combined with a ready tongue, a memory for scandal combined with wide acquaintance, approval of injustice combined with the ability to cover it up. This man combined all these vices. "Wherever he went, he formed a party; he beguiled the crowd with his hypocritical chatter; by his stubborn opposition to it, he perverted the law and furthered only his own designs. When scoundrels band together, that is ground for dismay."

Confucius was the butt of much criticism. It was said that to master his teachings no lifetime could be long enough; that they were of no use to the people; that he was incapable of sound administration and practical work; that he would impoverish the state with elaborate funerals; that he was nothing but a man of letters, traveling about, dispensing advice, leading the life of a parasite; that he was haughty and overbearing, trying to impress the multitude with ornate dress and affected manners.

B. Legend tells how as a young man he went to see the aged Lao-tzu. Lao-tzu did not approve of his activity of planning, advising, and studying. Books are questionable, they are but the footprints of the ancient sages. They made the footprints, whereas people today only talk. "All your lectures," Lao-tzu is reported to have said, "are concerned with things that are no better than footprints in the dust." "What you are reading can be nothing but the lees and scum of bygone men. . . . All that was worth handing on, died with them; the rest, they put in their books."

The essential, said Lao-tzu, was fundamental knowledge, and he reproached Confucius for his ignorance of the *tao*. Confucius, he declared, was misled by his ethical absolutes. Justice and love of humanity are mere consequences for one who loves the *tao;* in themselves they are nothing. When Confucius demands impartial love for all men, Lao tzu answers sharply:

To speak of "loving all men" is a foolish exaggeration, and to make up one's mind to be impartial is in itself a kind of partiality. . . . You had best study how it is that Heaven and Earth maintain their eternal course, that the sun and moon maintain their light, the stars their serried ranks, the birds and beasts their flocks, the trees and shrubs their station. Thus you too shall learn to guide your steps by Inward Power, to follow the course that the Way of Nature sets; and soon you will reach a goal where you will no longer need to go round laboriously advertising goodness and duty. . . . All this talk of goodness and duty, these perpetual pin-pricks unnerve and irritate the hearer. . . . The swan does not need a daily bath in order to remain white.[1]

Only in nonaction (*wu-wei*) is the *tao* revealed; everything else is superficial. Mere morality without a grounding in the *tao* is contrary to man's nature. But if the world in the *tao*, i.e., natural simplicity, is not lost, manners will spring up of their own accord, virtue will be set in motion.

Only "when the great *tao* fell into disregard, did benevolence and justice arise; when knowledge and cunning appeared, the great artificiality came into being." When the source of the *tao* dries up, men take to the expedients of humanity and justice but in vain. It is as with the fish: "When the pool dries up, fish makes room for fish upon the dry land, they moisten one another with damp breath, spray one another with foam from the jaws. But how much better are they off when they can forget one another, in the freedom of river and lake!"[2] Hence the right way is for men to live simply in the *tao* without artifice and constraint, without thought or knowledge of good and evil. "In antiquity adherence to the *tao* was not used to enlighten the people but to keep them in ignorance."

Lao-tzu is held to be Confucius' one real adversary. But the later polemics between Taoists and Confucians cast their shadows on these legendary conversations. The hostile parties of later days were both far removed from the origins. The later Taoists shunned the world, they were ascetics, conjurers, alchemists, prolongers of life, magicians, and charlatans. The later Confucians were men of the world, practical politicians adapting themselves to its ways, dry legalists, self-seeking and hungry for power.

An examination of the facts and the central attitudes of the two great philosophers suggests that while Lao-tzu and Confucius were indeed contrary poles, they presuppose one another and form a single whole. The narrowness of Confucianism should not be ascribed to Confucius. It is often held that Lao-tzu conceived the *tao* as beyond good and evil, while Confucius moralized the *tao*. But it is more accurate to say that when Confucius enters on the worldly task of creating order in the community through knowledge of good and evil, he leaves the realm beyond good and evil

[1] Tr. Arthur Waley.
[2] Tr. Arthur Waley.

strictly intact. For he does not take the community as an absolute. For him the Encompassing is a background, not a theme to work with; it is the limit and foundation to be considered with awe, not the immediate task. The essential difference is the difference between Lao-tzu's direct way to the *tao* and Confucius' detour by way of the human order, hence the divergent practical consequences of the same fundamental view.

The *tao* which Lao-tzu puts before and above everything else is for Confucius the One. But Lao-tzu immerses himself in it, while Confucius lets himself be guided by his awe of the One as he moves among the things of the world. At times Confucius also shows a tendency to shun the world; at the limits he too discloses the notion of acting by inaction and so keeping the world in order. Though the two philosophers look in opposite directions, they stand on the same ground. Their unity has been embodied by great historic figures, not in a philosophy that systematically embraced both sets of teachings, but in the Chinese wisdom of a life illumined by thought.

8. INFLUENCE

In his day Confucius was only one among many philosophers and by no means the most successful. But from him grew Confucianism, which for two thousand years, down to the end of the Empire in 1911, was the dominant force in Chinese thought.

The development of Confucianism falls roughly into the following stages.

1. In the centuries after Confucius, Mencius (c. 372–289 B.C.) and Hsün Tzŭ (c. 310–230) developed an effective scholastic tradition and codified the principles of Confucianism. Confucian thinking became more abstract, precise, systematic. The most beautiful and clearest formulations in the spirit of Confucius are to be found in the *Tai hsiao* and the *Chung-Yung*. The maxims of the *Lun-Yü,* closer to Confucius and perhaps in part taken literally from him, are short, fragmentary, rich in possibilities of interpretation. They are ideas in *statu nascendi,* like those of certain pre-Socratics, complete in themselves but offering infinite possibilities of development. When they were put into systematic form, the conceptual structure was enriched, but inevitably the fullness of the source was diminished. In the work of his immediate successors, Confucius became clearer but at the same time more limited. This Confucianism was a cultural movement, carried on by literary men with political pretensions. The Emperor Ch'in-shih-Huang-ti attempted to destroy it. The Confucian books were burned, and every effort was made to put an end to the tradition. After the great despot's death (210 B.C.) his dynasty was overthrown in a fierce civil war. But his work remained: the transformation of the old feudal state into a centralized bureaucracy.

2. Now an amazing thing happened: Under the Han dynasty (206 B.C.–

A.D. 220) the new bureaucratic state established by the despot made an alliance with Confucianism. Thus the new conception of state power, which drew its authority from the Confucian spirit, developed in part from situations and motives that were foreign to Confucius himself. He had known nothing other than the feudal state. Risen to actual power, Confucianism now acquired a new intellectual form. The men of letters became functionaries in the bureaucracy. Partly in the interest of their class, they developed an orthodoxy bordering on fanaticism. The doctrine became a system for the training of officials. The Confucian schools became state schools, serving to inculcate methods of government and to sanctify the state.

3. The Sung period (960–1276) witnessed a many-sided development, particularly in the directions of metaphysics and natural philosophy. At the same time, an orthodox canon was established on the foundation laid by Mencius. In the Manchu period (1644–1911), Confucian orthodoxy was further intensified and achieved its ultimate dogmatic form. This cultural congealment has largely determined the Western picture of China. Europeans long accepted the Chinese belief that their country had been the same since time immemorial, until the Sinologists unearthed the magnificent reality of Chinese history.

Thus Confucianism, like Christianity and Buddhism, underwent many transformations in the course of a long history. By the time of its official and general acceptance, it was far removed from its source in Confucius himself. Its history was a struggle, spiritually for the orthodox doctrine, politically for the domination of the lettered caste. In large part, the great artistic, literary, philosophical movements that mark the cultural history of China had to break through the barrier of this Confucianism, though their opposition to it was not always conscious. When cultural life was at an ebb, Confucianism—like Catholicism in the West—was always there to fall back on. But it too had its spiritual peaks; just as Catholicism had its St. Thomas, so Confucianism had its Chu Hsi (1131–1200).

Every higher impulse brings its own dangers. The centuries-long degeneration of Confucianism has led many observers—quite wrongly—to look for it in the source. They argue that Confucius' thinking is "reactionary," that it absolutizes the past, that it fixates and kills, that because it envisages no future, it paralyzes all creative, living, progressive forces.

As far as Confucius is concerned, this view is refuted by the clear maxims we have attempted to accentuate and place in their all-encompassing context. And there are many Confucians to whom it does not apply. But in regard to Confucianism in general, it is borne out by the regression that took place over the centuries. It may be characterized as follows:

1. The idea of the unknowable One is transformed into metaphysical indifference. When Confucius declines to think about the absolute or to pray for help, it is because a certainty rooted in the Encompassing enjoins him to turn to mankind in the actual world. By living in serene acceptance of death,

not asking to know what we cannot know, he leaves everything open. But once Confucius' certainty is lacking, skepticism runs rampant and with it an uncontrolled superstition. Agnosticism becomes a vacuum, which Confucianism seeks to fill with material magic and illusionary expectations.

2. Confucius' simple but passionate drive toward humanity is transformed into utilitarian thinking. The result is a pedantic pragmatism shorn of any feeling for man's independent worth.

3. The free ethos, implied by the polarity between the *li* and the power that guides them, is transformed into a dogmatization of the *li*. Without their ground in the *jên* and in the One, the *li* become mere rules of external behavior. While in Confucius they are a mild power, they now become rigid forms, laws enforced by coercion. They are woven into a complicated system of virtues and regulations, binding and immobilizing all human relations.

4. Openness of thought degenerates into dogmatic theory. For example, a controversy arises as to whether man is good or evil by nature, whether training in the *li* makes man good or only restores him to his true nature. Confucius saw no such alternatives; apart from the extremes, the saint and the fool who were immutable, men were free to develop their potentialities; let practice decide. But now theory became a hotly contested battlefield. And these theoretical alternatives, which for Confucius would have paled to insignificance beside that which transcends them, led nowhere.

5. The knowledge that was inner action degenerates into rote learning. There arose the class of scribes who distinguished themselves not by personality but by formal learning and maintained their prestige by a system of examinations. For Confucius antiquity was a norm which each man must acquire for himself. As transformed in Confucianism, this came to mean the study of ancient works, the pre-eminence of the scholar; instead of making antiquity his own, the student learned to imitate it. School learning produced an orthodoxy which lost its bond with life as a whole.

But despite its vast effects in Chinese history, this process of degeneration could not completely obscure the source. Confucius himself remained alive and his person played an important role in the whole development of Confucianism. Always men's eyes were turned toward him, the one great authority. We are told that his disciples felt free to criticize his actions but looked up to him as "to the sun and the moon, without which one cannot live." In line with the ancestor cult, sacrifices were offered at his tomb. Later a temple was built. As early as the end of the second century B.C. the historian Ssŭ-ma Ch'ien wrote of a visit to Confucius' tomb: "Filled with veneration I lingered and could hardly tear myself away. On earth there have been many princes and sages, famous during their lifetime, but all was over with them at their death. Confucius was a simple man of the people. But his teachings have been handed down for ten generations. Beginning with the Son of Heaven, with kings and princes, all take their decisions and their measure from the master. Surely this is highest sanctity." Later, temples were erected throughout the Chinese Empire. At the beginning of the twentieth century Confucius was expressly declared to be a god. It is a memorable development which ultimately made a god of this man who wished to be nothing but a man and knew that he was not even a saint.

JESUS

Though it is not possible to base a portrait of Jesus on compelling historic proof, his reality is clearly discernible through the veil of tradition. Unless we are willing to trust the fragmentary tradition and run the risk of error, we shall be left with a mere critical investigation that dispels every shred of reality. We must start with our personal engagement in the story of Jesus. Then, working with the findings of scholarship, we shall attempt to gather the data that are reliable, probable, or merely possible, and shape them into a picture. Such a portrait will be grounded in our own human relation to Jesus the man. Through the obscuring veils we shall attempt to arrive at the real figure, to perceive what kind of man he was, what he did, and what he said.

1. THE MESSAGE

What we know most certainly of Jesus is his message: the coming of the kingdom of heaven, what men must do to prepare for it, salvation through faith.

A. *The end of the world and the kingdom of heaven:* The thought and action of Jesus presuppose the forthcoming end of the world (Schweitzer, Martin Werner). It is seen as a catastrophe. "For in those days shall be affliction, such as was not from the beginning of the creation . . . neither shall be"; ". . . the sun shall be darkened, and the moon shall not give her light, and the stars of heaven shall fall."

Here Jesus merely accepted the prevailing apocalyptic conceptions. But he was in utter earnest. The end of the world was imminent. "Verily I say unto you, that this generation shall not pass, till all these things be done." "Verily I say unto you, there be some standing here, which shall not taste of death, till they see the Son of man coming in his kingdom." In sending out the disciples to announce the impending event, Jesus says: "Ye shall not have gone over the cities of Israel, till the Son of man be come." Unlike most of the apocalyptic preachers of his time, Jesus had little to say of the terrors of the end. But because for him this event, usually regarded as far off, was imminent, he believed it to be the inexorable concern of every living man. In the face of it, everything else paled to insignificance. Whatever remains for me to do can take on meaning only in the light of this end.

And a meaning is possible. For the end of the world will bring not nothingness but the kingdom of heaven. The kingdom of heaven: this signifies the era in which God alone will govern. Inevitably it will come, not through any human acts but solely through divine action. The world has become a matter of indifference, because the kingdom of heaven is coming in all its glory. Hence the happy tidings: "Blessed are the poor in spirit, for theirs is the kingdom of heaven." And "Fear not, little flock; for it is your Father's good pleasure to give you the kingdom." And the prayer: "Thy kingdom come." Thus the end is not only a threat, the destruction of the world, but also a promise: the kingdom of God. The mood is one of mingled dread and jubilation.

This prophecy of world's end and kingdom of heaven relates to a cosmic event. But it is not an event in the world, such as might give rise to a new world; rather, it is the event by which the world ceases to be, an intervention in history, whereby history is broken off. The kingdom of God is neither world nor history, nor is it this world's hereafter. It is something entirely different.

But the tidings of the kingdom carry a strange ambiguity. The kingdom will come and it is already here. What the future will fulfill is already at work in the world. This thought is expressed in the image of the mustard seed, for the mustard seed is the smallest of seeds, but from it grows the largest of herbs. And so it is with the kingdom. But above all, it is stated in the words: "For behold, the kingdom of God is within you." That is to say, the signs of the kingdom, Jesus, his person, his acts, his message, are among you. Thus what is already present is not the kingdom but the signs of the kingdom, the signs of its imminence (Martin Dibelius). It is to these signs that Jesus refers in his reply to John the Baptist's question: "Art thou he that should come?" Jesus says neither yes nor no, but: "The blind see, the lame walk, the lepers are cleansed, the deaf hear, the dead are raised, to the poor the gospel is preached." And Jesus also says: "But if I cast out devils by the Spirit of God, then the kingdom of God is come unto you."

The acts of Jesus, which are those of all wonder workers, his behavior toward sinners, social outcasts, harlots, his words that stir the souls of his listeners: all these serve as signs and examples. His purpose is not to improve the world, not to reform men and their institutions, but to show all those who hear and see him that the kingdom of God is at hand.

He lives the brief moment "between the eras," between the existence of the world and the kingdom of God.

Jesus predicts what will happen. But he is not merely purveying news to an idle crowd. His message is addressed to man, who in this situation is confronted by a decision. The message is: "The time is fulfilled, and the kingdom of God is at hand: repent ye, and believe the gospel." "Repent, do penance," therein lies the answer to the question: What shall we do, what can have meaning, if the world is about to end?

The kingdom does not mean beatitude for all. Each individual is faced with the question of what will become of him in the catastrophe. For the end of the world is also a judgment, in which man is either accepted or rejected by God. "Then shall two be in the field; the one shall be taken, and the other left."

The end of the world and the last judgment are not yet. But they may come at any moment. They will come suddenly like the lightning that flashes from east to west, or the thief in the night, or the master who returns home unbeknown to his servants. "But of that day and hour knoweth no man, no, not the angels of heaven, but my Father only."

Jesus bids those who are forewarned to live in readiness: "Watch ye therefore; for ye know not when the master of the house cometh . . . lest coming suddenly he find you sleeping." Watch—and wait. For man can do nothing to bring the kingdom. It will come of itself, by God's will alone. As the husbandman waits for the harvest, so man for the kingdom. And he bids them to divulge the tidings. In your preaching, announce the catastrophe and the glad news to all, that they may be saved.

B. *The ethos:* In telling men what to do, Jesus is not promulgating a self-sufficient system of ethics for the fulfillment of mankind in the structure and order of worldly existence. On the contrary, ethical precepts are justified only by the will of God, who has given them as a sign of the kingdom and preparation for the end.

Worldly things have lost all weight of their own. "The world is only a bridge; cross it, but build not thy house upon it." The world is indeed God's creation and as such should not be condemned. Jesus loved nature like Francis of Assisi after him. He accepts the human order and insists on the validity of its ordinances. The marriage bond is indissoluble: "What therefore God hath joined together, let not man put asunder." Nor should men rebel against the authorities: "Render to Caesar the things that are Caesar's, and to God the things that are God's." But all worldly existence dwindles to nothingness in the radiance of the kingdom of heaven. Family ties, law, culture have lost their meaning. His mother and brothers wait for him in vain: "For whosoever shall do the will of my Father which is in heaven, the same is my brother, and sister, and mother." Possessions are an encumbrance; the young man who knows that with all his fulfillment of the commandments he is not with God, is advised to sell all he has and give to the poor.

All worldly things are perishable. "Which of you by taking thought can add one cubit unto his stature?" And: "Sufficient unto the day is the evil thereof." But the world is not worthy of our concern. "Take no thought for your life, what ye shall eat, or what ye shall drink." "Take no thought for the morrow: for the morrow shall take thought for the things of itself." Only what has reality in the kingdom of heaven is important: "Lay not up for yourselves treasures upon earth, where moth and rust doth corrupt, . . . But lay up for yourselves treasures in heaven."

What is this one important thing? Each man is faced with the terrible alternative: to be accepted in the kingdom of heaven or rejected. There are God and the devil, the angels and the demons, good and evil. For each man everything depends on his decision: which way will he turn? This either-or is addressed to every individual: "And if thy hand offend thee, cut it off: it is better for thee to enter into life maimed, than having two hands to go into hell." "No man can serve two masters. . . . Ye cannot serve God and mammon." There is no in-between, no compromise, only all or nothing. There remains only one imperative: follow God and so enter into the eternity of His kingdom.

Obedience to God was the ethos of the Jew Jesus as it had always been the ethos of the Jews. But external, calculable obedience to definite laws is not enough. The essential is the obedience of man's whole heart and being. For as Jeremiah said, God has written his law in the heart of man.

But what is God's will? Our thinking, accustomed as it is to the finite rules of the understanding, would like to have instructions, regulations to go by. The understanding may ask God in defiance: What is Thy will? When we hear the commandments that Jesus uttered as God's will, we are startled at their extremism: they demand something that is impossible in the world. But these commandments state what can become real in the kingdom of heaven: "Be ye therefore perfect, even as your Father which is in heaven is perfect." They are addressed to a man who knows only God and his neighbor and acts as though there were no world, as though the antinomies of worldly reality did not exist. These imperatives assume that man no longer has any finite situation in the world, or mission to shape and fulfill the world; they are imperatives for saints, for citizens of the kingdom of heaven: "But I say unto you, That ye resist not evil: but whosoever shall smite thee on thy right cheek, turn to him the other also. And if any man will sue thee at the law, and take away thy coat, let him have thy cloak also. . . . Give to him that asketh thee, and from him that would borrow of thee turn not thou away."

Above all, they are not imperatives of outward action, but imperatives that penetrate the innermost soul prior to all action. The soul must be pure. Even in the secret recesses of the soul the germ of evil is as reprehensible as the outward action: "Whosoever looketh on a woman to lust after her hath committed adultery with her already in his heart."

What Jesus demands is a mode of being, not an outward action, which merely follows from the being. He demands what cannot be willed but is the source of all willing. Where it is present, no power in the world can darken it. "Not that which goeth into the mouth defileth a man; but that which cometh out of the mouth, this defileth a man."

God's will is the life of the kingdom of heaven—live as though the kingdom of heaven were already with us; so live that this life in the world will become a sign of the kingdom of heaven and indeed its approaching reality.

Jesus' ethos should not be taken as a system of prescriptions for action in this world. The principle springs solely from the idea of the kingdom of heaven, and Jesus uttered this principle in Biblical style: Thou shalt love the Lord thy God . . . and love thy neighbor as thyself. These commandments are a part of the old Jewish religion. "And thou shalt love the Lord thy God with all thine heart, and with all thy soul, and with all thy might." "Thou shalt love thy neighbor as thyself." "What doth the Lord require of thee, but to do justly, and to love mercy, and to walk humbly with thy God?" Here Jesus brings out nothing new. There is no prefatory "But I say unto you . . ." as when he is in disagreement with the traditional faith. He takes the traditional commandments with him into the kingdom of heaven announced in the reality of love that is the sign of its coming.

A mystical union with God, flight from the world to live alone among men, at one with God: that would be loveless. The individual for himself alone has no part in the kingdom of heaven. He must make his way thither with his neighbor. He who loves God loves his neighbor. Therefore life in the world is fulfilled by a life of love, which is the sign of the kingdom of heaven.

God's love of man and man's love of his neighbor are inseparable. Only insofar as we love can we know God's love. God's love creates love within us. If we do not love, we are rejected.

Where love has become selfless and free from the world, it is the reality of the kingdom of heaven. Then it is unlimited, absolute. Thence Jesus' new commandment, alien to the Old Testament, to love your enemies, to requite evil with good. "Love your enemies, bless them that curse you, do good to them that hate you, and pray for them which despitefully use you."

This love, then, is not a universal feeling without an object; it is a love of my neighbor. But who is my neighbor? Not my kinsman or one who is distinguished in some way, but everyone who is close to me in space and time and who needs me. This is made clear by the story of the good Samaritan. A man of Jerusalem lies half dead by the wayside, having been set upon by robbers. A priest comes that way, then a Levite, and both pass him by. But then a Samaritan, of a people despised in Jerusalem, sees him and has compassion for him and cares for him. "Which now of these three, thinkest thou, was neighbor unto him that fell among the thieves?" This kind of love precludes all self-aggrandizement. "He that is greatest among you shall be your servant, and whosoever shall exalt himself shall be abased." And it implies wholehearted devotion to Jesus and his calling: "He who loveth father and mother more than me is not worthy of me; . . . and he that taketh not his cross, and followeth after me, is not worthy of me."

This perfect love that is a sign of the kingdom is not satisfied by obedience to laws, by the pursuit of any plan or purpose. Jesus rejects legalism, not for the sake of lawlessness, but in order to seek the source whence the law flows and whereby it is fulfilled beyond all legality. He accepts the traditional law of the Old Testament as self-evident. He does not oppose it in principle as St. Paul was to do. But fulfillment of any definite law is far less important than a life of obedience to God: "The sabbath was made for man, and not man for the sabbath." Observance of rites cannot compensate for ethical offenses: "Therefore if thou bring thy gift to the altar, and there rememberest that thy brother hath ought against thee; leave there thy gift before the altar, and go thy way; first be reconciled to thy brother, and then come and offer thy gift."

Mere legality fosters hypocrisy. One who lives by the law alone masks the evil that is in him. To those who observe the law but have lost the inward faith, Jesus says: "Full well ye reject the commandment of God, that ye may keep your own tradition." And he warns the people against the scribes who "love to go in long clothing, and love salutations in the marketplaces, and the chief seats in the synagogues," who "devour widows' houses, and for a pretence make long prayers."

Thus the freedom of Jesus' actions is an essential part of this ethos of the kingdom, a freedom which is grounded not in law but in love. No true law is destroyed by love, for love will merely cushion it and keep it within bounds. This explains why Jesus did many things that offended those about him. He attended a marriage feast. He justified the woman who wasted expensive oil in anointing his feet: "She hath wrought a good work on me." He spoke with harlots and forgave the sinner who had faith: "for she loved much."

Jesus put forward no new system of morality but purified the Biblical ethos and took it as seriously as if it were already fulfilled in God's kingdom. He lived it without regard for the consequences in the world, for the world was soon to perish.

c. *The faith:* The end of the message is: Believe in the good tidings. Have faith (*pistis*). Faith is indispensable for admission to the kingdom of heaven. It is the prerequisite of salvation and is itself salvation.

Only to faith is the coming of the kingdom manifested. By the clouds men know that rain is coming, by the leaves of the fig tree they know that summer is nigh at hand; but they see not the signs of the coming kingdom. That is to say: they do not believe. The true sign is Jesus himself, his acts and his message. Only faith can see Jesus. Therefore: "Blessed is he, whosoever shall not be offended in me."

Faith is the life of those who have already glimpsed the kingdom of heaven. On this faith the most unbelievable gifts are bestowed: "All things are possible to him that believeth." "Whosoever shall say unto this mountain, Be thou removed and be thou cast into the sea; and shall not doubt in his heart, but shall believe that those things which he saith shall come to pass; he shall have whatsoever he saith." Jesus heals the sick, but his success is due to their faith: "Thy faith hath made thee whole." Jesus healed by the kind of suggestion that has been used all over the world to banish or induce certain abnormal phenomena. Only one who "believes" can experience such effects, which are familiar to our medical and psychological experience. But Jesus does more than perform miracles by suggestion: he forgives sins. To the sufferer from palsy he says: "Thy sins be forgiven thee." This he says because he has seen the sick man's faith. He cures him in order that men, seeing his power to cure, may be convinced of his power to forgive sins.

Those who believe in the kingdom of heaven know that God does not refuse the suppliant. Even men do not deny urgent prayer; the father does not give his hungry son a stone; the judge gives the widow her due. But far more than evil men will God give ear when men pray to Him. Therefore: "Ask, and it shall be given you; seek, and ye shall find; knock, and it shall be opened unto you."

But man should accept all this as a gift, knowing that he has not deserved it: "When ye shall have done all those things which are commanded you, say: We are unprofitable servants; we have done that which was our duty to do."

Thus man cannot keep accounts with God. God "maketh his sun to rise on the evil and on the good, and sendeth rain on the just and on the unjust." Human thought cannot undermine faith by figuring out what ought to happen. "With God all things are possible." Whatever happens, God knows why, and the believer finds no grievance against God in an unexpected catastrophe or in events that he simply cannot understand. Jesus is not Job.

This faith is expressed in the "Our Father." Three phrases are crucial: "Thy kingdom come"—in the kingdom we shall be one with God's will, the world will be ended and with it all affliction. "Give us this day our daily bread"—freedom from worldly cares is possible only through the faith that builds on God. "Forgive us our trespasses; and lead us not into temptation"—freedom from sins is the way to the kingdom of heaven, and freedom from sin can be given only by God.

For the believer, God is all in all. The finite and transient world is only a sign. But God makes the lilies grow in the field, no sparrow falls to the ground except by His will, the hairs of a man's head are numbered. Though sign and reality are interwoven, the metaphoric character of all worldly existence implies a radical separation between the world and the kingdom of heaven. The world passeth away, the kingdom abideth forever.

Faith is a word for the Biblical relation to God. It means absolute trust in the will of God. "Thy will be done" is an expression of this trust. Faith is certainty, concerning God, concerning man's bond with Him, concerning God's love which is the foundation of prayer. Faith is the salt that seasons a man's whole being. But it cannot be taken for granted, induced by design. It does not understand itself. It is weak and fragile. Effort can only denature it. It is a gift, not a possession. "Lord, I believe; help thou mine unbelief."

D. *Jesus' manner of communication:* Jesus preaches not knowledge but faith. His meaning remains veiled for the unbeliever; to the believer it is revealed, yet even then not in clear statements, but in parables and paradoxes. Questioned about the parables, he replies: "Unto you it is given to know the mystery of the kingdom of God; but unto them that are without, all these things are done in parables."

Jesus speaks in concrete terms, expresses intelligible ideas, utters definite commandments. Without this, effective communication would be impossible. But all his direct statements are vehicles of a meaning which ultimately evades rational interpretation.

Jesus shows little concern for logical consistency. He says, for example: "He that is not with me is against me." But: "For he that is not against us is on our part." Or on the one hand: "Resist not evil" and on the other: "I bring not peace but a sword." Where everything is a sign, there are no contradictions. His utterances do not represent a system of thought, but a message in signs.

2. LIFE

Jesus grew up in Nazareth in Galilee with his mother Mary, four brothers, and several sisters. He learned a trade. He must have received rabbinical instruction in the Old Testament. Grown to manhood, he heard of John the Baptist, the anchorite of the Jordan country, who proclaimed the coming of the kingdom and God's last judgment, and preached repentance, baptism, and the remission of sins. Jesus sought out John and having been baptized went into the desert. On his return he preached to the people. When he was about thirty, he spoke in the synagogues, was addressed as Rabbi, wandered from place to place in Galilee, gathered disciples around him, preached the end of the world and the coming of the kingdom. He became known as a performer of miracles, who healed the sick, drove out devils, and awakened the dead. He preached a life of indifference to the world, devoted to God's will and the ethos of love. His friends regarded him as a madman.

His career as a preacher lasted perhaps only a few months and at most three years. Only the last few days, comprising the Passion (A.D. 30 or 33), are described in detail, the main episodes being the journey to Jerusalem, the cleansing of the Temple, the Last Supper, the agony in the garden, the be-

trayal and arrest, the hearings, the judgment of the Sanhedrin, the decision
of Pontius Pilate, the crucifixion and burial.

The question arises: Why did Jesus go to Jerusalem? He was accompanied
by a multitude, a popular movement. His entrance into Jerusalem was an
event. The authorities were reminded of the disorders that had been created
by other agitators and quelled by force. Jesus, to be sure, showed no sign of
any desire for political power. Yet the atmosphere suggests that he wished
to provoke some sort of decision. But what decision? One theory is that,
expecting the kingdom of heaven to set in at any moment, he wished to
preach the gospel at the feast of the Passover in Jerusalem, the center of
Jewish life, in order to reach as many souls as possible for their salvation.
Another is that, disappointed that the world was taking so long to end and
identifying himself with the servant of God in Deutero-Isaiah, Jesus had
come to believe that God demanded his martyrdom at the hand of the
worldly powers and that with this event He would usher in the kingdom
of heaven. It has been suggested that Jesus on the cross expected the kingdom
to dawn at the last moment and gave vent to his final disillusionment by
crying: "My God, my God, why hast thou forsaken me?" But these are mere
suppositions. All we know for certain is that Jesus went up to Jerusalem and
preached there—and that a popular movement formed around him.

His conduct is not explained by thoughtlessness; he did not go blindly
to his doom. In speaking to his disciples, he counseled prudence: "I send
you forth as sheep in the midst of wolves; be ye therefore wise as serpents,
and harmless as doves." And still more clearly: "Give not that which is
holy unto the dogs, neither cast ye your pearls before swine, lest they trample
them under their feet, and turn again and rend you." In his wanderings in
Galilee, Jesus kept as hidden as possible when it seemed likely that Herod,
in his alarm, would seek to destroy him as he had destroyed other prophets.
In Jerusalem he took care to avoid traps. To those who tried to compromise
him with the Romans or the Jews by asking what he thought about the pay-
ment of tribute, he replied shrewdly, pointing to the effigy on a coin:
"Render to Caesar the things that are Caesar's and to God the things that
are God's." Since the authorities did not dare to arrest him by day, when
he was always surrounded by the multitude, they sought him by night and
then he hid, always in different places. He does not seem to have made up
his mind what to do in case of arrest, whether resistance should be offered;
in any event the disciples were uncertain. He tells them to buy swords. But
when taken, he does not resist. When one of the apostles smites the servant
of the high priest and cuts off his ear, Jesus does not reprove him, but bids
him hold his peace.

His actions in Jerusalem were perfectly open. The entrance into the city
must have been prepared. He purified the Temple on the strength of the
position he claimed in the Jewish community. To the Sanhedrin he was a
rebel against the Jewish theocracy and a blasphemer. The Romans suspected

him of political insurrection. Jesus himself avoided any statement of what he took himself to be. According to the Gospel, he makes such a statement only at the end. When the high priest asks him if he is the Christ, he replies: "I am," and to Pilate's question: "Art thou the King of the Jews?" he answers: "Thou sayest." According to the inscription on the cross, he was condemned to death as a pretender to the crown.

If Jesus was not an active political leader (like the so-called Zealots); if he desired no social revolution; if he did not seek a martyr's death as proof of his message; if he led the life of a believer, awaiting God's action but making no attempt to force God's hand; if he was far from any desire for self-aggrandizement, and his whole life was an act of obedience to God's will, his conduct becomes hard to understand. For by violence (cleansing of the Temple, creation of a movement among the people) he provoked violence against himself. What he suffered was the consequence of his act. In all this there is a flavor of militancy which is also unmistakable in other manifestations of his personality.

Jesus' view of himself is by no means clear. In his preaching he must have become aware of the discrepancy between what he himself was, saw, and strove for, and what others understood. The people followed him eagerly; in their way they needed him. He could not prevent them from attaching themselves to him and raising him more and more above himself. But the development of his picture of himself is not clear. The contradictions in his utterances only show that there was such a development and that perhaps it was never completed. Let us consider some of his sayings.

Such phrases as "I am come . . . ," "But I say unto you . . ." show an awareness of his vocation. Jesus makes it clear that he believed himself to be extraordinary by likening himself to light and fire: "I am come to send fire on the earth." When among those who had long known him he encountered an indifference or contempt that offended his sense of his own worth, he said: "No prophet is accepted in his own country."

He was surprised at their lack of faith and at his inability to perform miracles among them.

He surely believed in his calling to preach. He regarded himself as a prophet and perhaps in the end as the Messiah. This picture of himself was inevitably molded by the current conceptions of prophecy: the worldly and divine "king" descended from the house of David, who would rule in the last days; the angel who appears as the "son of Man" in Daniel's prophecy of the end of the world; the servant of God, the suffering, dying, rising Saviour of Deutero-Isaiah. All these conceptions are echoed in sayings of Jesus. He frequently speaks of himself as the Son of man. "The foxes have holes, and the birds of the air have nests; but the Son of man hath not where to lay his head." Something in his conduct in Jerusalem must have fostered the suspicion that he aspired to the crown, though his accusers no doubt misinterpreted his intentions.

Did Jesus definitely regard himself as the Messiah, the Christ? On the one hand, he did not wish to be spoken of as the Messiah and forbade those possessed by devils to address him as the son of David. He charged his disciples to tell no man that he was Jesus the Christ. But on the other hand: "He saith unto them, but whom say ye that I am? And Simon Peter answered and said, Thou art the Christ, the Son of the living God. And Jesus answered and said unto him, Blessed art thou, Simon Bar-jona: for flesh and blood hath not revealed it unto thee, but my Father which is in heaven." Certain of the sayings attributed to him show a theological tone that seems to brand them as inauthentic. For example: "All things are delivered unto me of my Father, and no man knoweth the Son, but the Father; neither knoweth any man the Father, save the Son, and he to whomsoever the Son will reveal him." But no Christian could have devised words such as: "Why callest thou me good? there is none good but one, that is, God." These must really have been spoken by Jesus.

Taken all together, the words of Jesus do not supply an unequivocal answer. He did not commit himself to dogmatic formulations and apparently came to no definite conclusion about the nature of his own person. The question itself seems to be a fallacy resulting from dogmatic bias.

The account of Jesus' life set forth in the Gospels contains episodes and words which historical criticism has correctly explained as transferences from the Old Testament. But in regard to a good many particulars, critical method cannot provide any certainty.

It is contended, for example, that the story of the agony in the garden could not have been an eyewitness account (for how could anyone have observed his vacillation, his struggle with his own weakness?), but, rather, a fiction calculated to confirm the fulfillment of God's will as revealed in the Old Testament. And Jesus' last words: "My God, my God, why hast thou forsaken me?" are interpreted according to the same method. After his death, it is explained, the Christians, drawing on the Old Testament, came to believe that Jesus had despaired and cried out in lamentation but had found consolation in prayer. Thus the last words are "not the cry of a despairing man but the beginning of the Twenty-second Psalm, and the man who prays in these words is not a rebel against God, but one who lives and dies at peace with God" (Martin Dibelius).

It would take very compelling reasons to make us abandon the belief that there is a reality at the base of these moving episodes. Jesus the man reveals himself in the purity of his soul and in his struggle with unexpected realities. The struggle culminates in no finished self-awareness or dogma. In the face of unexpected terrors, in the face of his mounting disappointment, all that was left him was his prayer: Thy will be done.

3. THE PERSONALITY OF JESUS

It is easy to say what Jesus was not. He was not a philosopher who reflects methodically and systematically orders his ideas. He was not a social reformer who makes plans; for he left the world as it was, it was about to end in any case. He was not a political leader aiming to overthrow one state and found another; he never uttered a single word about the events of his time. He founded no cult, for like the early Christians he participated in the Jewish cult; he did not baptize and he established no organization, no congregation, no church. What then was he?

There are three ways in which we may attempt to characterize Jesus: we may look at him psychologically, according to his individual reality, or historically, as part of a larger cultural context; or we may try to find his essential character in his idea.

A. *Possible psychological aspects:* In his *Antichrist,* Nietzsche describes Jesus as a psychological type, hypersensitive, prone to suffering and dreading it above all else. Thus reality was intolerable to him, he could accept it only as a parable, a sign. The world he lived in was not a real world, but a world of vague, intangible symbols.

Hostility, opposition, the resistance of concrete things were intolerable to him. For Nietzsche this explains why he did not contend with the world, and "resist not evil" is the key to the gospel. In this maxim Jesus' personal incapacity for struggle is set up as an ethical principle.

The only true reality is the inner reality, which is called life, truth, light. The kingdom of God is a psychological state. It is not expected, but is present everywhere and nowhere. It it a state of beatitude which cannot be demonstrated by miracles or by scripture, which offers no promise or reward, but is its own proof, its own miracle and reward. Its proofs are inner lights, feelings of pleasure and self-satisfaction. The problem is: How shall I live in order to feel that I am in heaven, at all times divine, the child of God? For this sense of beatitude is the sole reality.

Jesus is not a hero or a genius, but more in the nature of an idiot (Nietzsche apparently uses the word in much the same sense as Dostoevski). For Nietzsche the Jesus of the Sermon on the Mount with his Beatitudes is utterly incompatible with Jesus the fanatical militant, the deadly enemy of the priests and theologians. Consequently, he ascribes everything in the Gospels that does not suit his picture of Jesus to the invention of the early militant congregation, which required a militant prototype.

It is doubtful whether anyone will be convinced by Nietzsche's interpretation. The whole of Jesus cannot be found in Francis of Assisi. True, such features can be singled out of the Gospel narrative. But they are not the only ones. In the Gospels, Jesus appears as an elemental power, by turns unbendingly aggressive and infinitely gentle.

"He looked on them with anger," "he assailed him," "he rebuked him," "he menaced him." Finding no fruit on a fig tree, he withers it with his curse: no man should eat fruit of it forever thereafter. Those who do not do the will of the Father in heaven, Jesus will deny at the last judgment: I never knew you, depart from me. They are "cast into outer darkness," "there shall be weeping and gnashing of teeth." "Whosoever shall deny me before men, him will I also deny before my Father which is in heaven. Think not that I am come to send peace on earth; I came not to send peace, but a sword. For I am come to set a man at variance against his father, and the daughter against her mother." He reviles the cities that do not repent: "Woe unto thee, Chorazin; woe unto thee, Bethsaida! It shall be more tolerable for Tyre and Sidon at the day of judgment, than for you." When Peter is offended to hear that the Son of man will suffer much, be killed, and rise again, Jesus rebukes him: "Get thee behind me, Satan, . . . thou savourest not the things that be of God, but those that be of men." Violently, with a whip, he drives the money-changers from the Temple.

Jesus can simply not be interpreted as passive, mild, moved always and only by love, much less as a helpless neurasthenic.

The strange duality of gentleness and uncompromising militancy is evident in the words with which Jesus demands faith. He can say: "My yoke is easy, and my burden is light," but he can also command men to follow him at once, without hesitation, and without reservation. To the young man who wishes first to bury his father, he cries imperiously: "Follow me; and let the dead bury their dead." He curses the unbelievers in the words of Isaiah: "Ye shall hear, and shall not understand; for this people's heart was waxed gross." He gives thanks that God should have hidden the truth from the wise and prudent, and revealed it to babes.

B. *Historical aspects:* Jesus is a figure of late antiquity, living on the margin of the Hellenistic-Roman world. In a period of luminous history, he spent his life in obscurity, barely noticed by the outside world. What part could this man who did not calculate at all have in a calculating, realistic, rationalized world where nothing mattered but power? From the standpoint of all material reality, his life was a mistake and could only end in failure.

Compared to the archaic Jewish Prophets, who seem cast in bronze, he seems contemplative, ambiguous, and volatile. But compared with the Hellenistic-Roman world, he has the originality of a first beginning. Some have tried to explain Jesus as one of the many religious or political fanatics of his time. He has been identified with the apocalyptic movement that was widespread in the Near East, with such sects as the Essenes who sought salvation in a life of purity and serene brotherhood, or with the revolutionary movements proclaiming a Messiah who would restore the kingdom of Israel;

he has been numbered among the wandering prophets spoken of by Celsus, who went about the cities, temples, army camps, begging, telling fortunes, claiming to be sent by God to save other men and cursing those who would not acknowledge them; and he has been likened to the artisans who wandered about the desert with the Bedouins, destitute but carefree, watching their battles but taking no part, caring for the wounded on both sides, men of peace, living successfully among warriors.

Jesus may have something in common with all these types. Certain aspects of their lives and modes of thought provide a possible framework for his existence. But once this is recognized, the reality of Jesus shatters the framework, for it is utterly different in meaning, origin, and dignity. He reveals breadths and depths unknown to the others. All those who came forward as Messiahs were executed and forgotten; when they had failed, their followers ceased to believe in them. The religious fanatics lost themselves in particulars and externals. If so many heterogeneous types can cast a light on Jesus, it only goes to show that he belongs to none of them.

It has been said, rightly perhaps, that there was nothing new in the teachings of Jesus. He accepted the knowledge of those about him, worked with traditional ideas. The God that he loved so intensely was the Jewish God. It never occurred to him to break with the Jewish faith. Like the ancient Prophets, he lived in it, while opposing the congealed forms and dogmas of the priests. Historically, he is the last of the Jewish Prophets. He cites them often and explicitly.

But if only because of the changed world, there was a difference between Jesus and the ancient Prophets. They had lived in an independent Jewish state and witnessed its decline and end. Jesus lived in a long-stabilized and politically dependent Jewish theocracy. Between the political independence of the Jews and their final dispersion after the destruction of Jerusalem, there elapsed a period of five centuries marked by many of the most fervent Psalms, the Books of Ecclesiastes and Job—and the career of Jesus. The Jewish theocracy cast him out, as the priests in the days of the Kings had attempted to cast out the Prophets. The Talmudic Jews of the Diaspora who accepted the old Prophets as part of the canon could no longer accept Jesus, for in the meanwhile Gentiles had built a world religion around him.

Historically, Jesus' faith in God is one of the great creations of Jewish Biblical religion. The God of Jesus, the God of the Bible, is no longer one of the Oriental gods from whom Yahweh was descended. Gradually He had lost his Oriental cruelty and lust for offerings, largely through the Prophets who molded a more profound conception of sacrifice and spoke their last word in Jesus. Nor is this God one of the grandiose mythical figures who symbolized and so sublimated and guided the primordial forces of human existence, after the manner of Athene, Apollo, and all the rest; He is the imageless, formless One. Yet He is not a mere universal power; He is not the world reason of Greek philosophy, but an active person. Nor is He the unfathomable Being with which man achieves mystical union in meditation; He is the absolutely Other, which can be believed but not seen. He is absolute transcendence, before the world and outside of the world, and He is the creator of the world. In relation to the world and man, He is will: "He spoke, and it was done; He commanded, and it stood fast." Impenetrable in His decisions, He is trusted and obeyed without reserve. He is the judge who sees man's most hidden thoughts, and before whom man must give an accounting. He is the father who loves and forgives, in whose presence man knows himself to be a child of God. He is jealous and hard, but merciful and compassionate. Remote and unapproachable, He governs from afar, but He is close at hand, speaking in man's heart and communicating His imperatives. He is not mute and intangible like the One Being of speculation; rather, He is the living God who speaks directly to each man.

Jesus believed in the God of the Old Testament and fulfilled the old Prophetic religion. Like Jeremiah, he was a Jew, pure of heart, freed from all bonds of law, ritual, and cult. He did not reject all these forms, but subordinated them to the present will of God. Once again Jesus embodied the Prophetic faith, which sustained him as it had sustained men for centuries.

c. *The essential idea:* The life of Jesus seems illumined by the Godhead. At every moment he is close to God, and nothing has meaning for him but God and God's will. The idea of God is subject to no condition, but the norms it imposes subject everything else to their condition. It gives knowledge of the simple ground of all things.

The essence of this faith is freedom. For in this faith that speaks of God, the soul expands in the Encompassing. As it experiences gladness and woe in this world, it awakens to itself. Nothing that is merely finite, that is only world, can hold it captive. From devotion, from the trust that transcends understanding, it derives an infinite power: for in the sorrow of the vulnerable heart, in rending emotion, it can gain awareness that it is given to itself by God. By believing, man can become truly free.

The certainty of his faith in God made possible for Jesus an attitude of soul which in itself is incomprehensible. He lived in the world and partook of its temporal existence, but, moved by a profound unworldly source, he was unmoved by the world. In the world, he transcends the world. Even while his life was given to the world, he was somehow—invisibly and indemonstrably, doubting it in his very statements—independent of the world.

This independence amid immersion in the world is the source of Jesus' wonderful serenity. On the one hand, worldly things could no longer tempt him into finite absolutes; the worldly husks of knowledge could no longer beguile him into total knowledge, nor the rules and laws into calculable dogma. All these temptations shattered against the freedom of his faith in

God. On the other hand, his own being was open to the world, his eye was alive to all realities, and particularly to the souls of men, the depths of their hearts, which could conceal nothing from his insight.

Once the idea of God, however mysteriously, penetrates the soul, there comes a fear of losing Him and an unremitting impulse to do whatever might prevent God from disappearing. Hence Jesus' dictum: "Blessed are the pure of heart, for they shall see God."

But then something happened in Jesus which in the Old Testament is present only in germ. In him the earnestness of the idea of God brought the most radical consequences. This God who for Jesus was not physically present—not in visions and not in voices—was able to put absolutely everything in the world in question. Everything in the world was drawn before His judgment seat. It is terrifying to see how this was done by Jesus in the certainty of his faith in God. Anyone who can read this in the synoptic Gospels and yet remain easy in his mind, content with his existence and caught up in its routines, is blind. Jesus broke free from every practical order in the world. He saw that all orders and habits had become pharisaical; he points to the source in which they melt to nothingness. All earthly reality is deprived of its foundation, absolutely and definitively. All orders whatsoever, the bonds of piety, of law, of reasonable custom, collapse. Beside the commandment to follow God into the kingdom of heaven, all other tasks—the earning of bread, the oath before the law, the claims of justice and property—become meaningless. To die at the hands of the powers of this world, in suffering, persecution, abuse, degradation, that is what befits the believer. "Never have words so revolutionary been spoken, for everything otherwise looked on as valid is represented as indifferent, unworthy of consideration" (Hegel).

Because Jesus stands at the end and margin of the world, in an exceptional situation, he reveals the possibility and hope implicit in all those who are despised according to the standards of the world, the lowly, the sick, the deformed, in all those who are banished from the orders of the world; he reveals the potentialities of man himself under any conditions. He points to the place where a home is open to man in every mode of failure.

Jesus made his way to this place where everything that is world is overshadowed. Metaphorically speaking, it is light and fire; directly, it is love and God. Conceived as a place in the world, it is not a place at all. By the standards of what is appropriate in the world, everyone is bound to misunderstand it. From the standpoint of the world it is impossible.

In the world, Jesus can point only indirectly to this source. He seems to test what is madness in the world for its possible truth. Both his actions and his words seem contradictory by the standards of reason: on the one hand, struggle, hardness, the ruthless alternative; on the other, infinite mildness, nonresistance, compassion with all the forlorn. He is the challenging warrior and the silent sufferer.

The radical certainty of his faith in God derived an unprecedented intensity from his expectation of the impending catastrophe. From the standpoint of cosmic knowledge, this expectation was error. But even if the world did not end, the fundamental idea retains its meaning. Whether immediately or far in the future, the end casts light and shade, puts its question to each and every man, summons him to decision. His mistaken belief in the physical end of the world brought the truth to light by compelling him to live in the presence of the catastrophe. For though men close their eyes to the ultimate, they are faced with it none the less. The world is not the first and last; man is doomed to die, mankind itself will not endure forever. In this situation the alternative is: with God or against God; good or evil. Jesus reminds men of this extreme situation.

An intrinsic element in the idea of Jesus is suffering, terrible, limitless suffering, crowned by the most cruel of deaths. His experience of suffering is the Jewish experience of suffering. His words on the cross, "My God, my God, why hast thou forsaken me?" are the opening of the Twenty-second Psalm. In his extreme suffering these were the words that came to his lips. In this Psalm a man speaks from the depths of affliction: "I am a worm and no man; a reproach of men, despised of the people." "O my God, I cry in the daytime, but thou hearest not." He is helpless and forsaken, and God is mute. And then, in the midst of his silence and despair, everything changes: "But thou art holy . . . our fathers trusted in thee."

The authenticity of Jesus' suffering is historically unique. The pain and terror are not accepted with resignation or borne with patience; they are not veiled. He insists on the reality of suffering and expresses it. When, forlorn and forsaken, he is nearly dead with suffering, the minimum of ground he has to stand on becomes all and everything, the Godhead. Silent, invisible, unimaginable, it is after all the sole reality. The utter realism with which the uncloaked horrors of this existence are portrayed implies that help can come only from the utterly intangible.

By the standard of a heroic or Stoic ethos there is no "dignity" in this forlorn despair or in the expression of it or in the sustaining ground that makes itself felt in the end as though by a miracle. Yet in extreme situations the ethos of dignity fails, or freezes into indifference.

Jesus is a summit of this power to suffer. To discern the essence of Jesus, we must know the essence of the Jews down through the centuries. But Jesus did not suffer passively. He acted, in order that his suffering and death should be a goad to men. He bared his absolute to a world that accepts only contingency and to the worldliness of the Church (that is, the Jewish theocracy that set its stamp on the churches of a later day). His reality is courage, above all in the fulfillment of his divine mission to tell the truth, to be the truth. That is the courage of the Jewish Prophets: not a courage to be mirrored in the fame of great deeds and a brave death for posterity, but before God alone. In the crucifixion the fundamental reality of the eternal is embodied in time. In the traditional symbol of the cross, man gained certainty of the authentic amid the failure of everything that is world.

The Jewish experience of suffering is an element of the Old Testament religion, which is the kernel of all Christian, Jewish, Islamic religions in all their innumerable historical forms, deviations, perversions, so that none of them can claim to be in possession of the true Biblical religion, which nevertheless sustains them all. It is impossible to speak directly of the Biblical religion without making dangerous claims. But perhaps we may say this: Christ, a creation of the early Christian congregation and of St. Paul, is not, any more than the Jewish law or the national character of the Jewish and many Protestant religions, a common factor in all Biblical religion. Common factors are: the idea of God, and, insofar as Jesus was the last embodiment of the Jewish idea of the suffering servant of God, the cross.

4. THE INFLUENCE OF JESUS

It is boundless. Here I can give only a few indications.

A. *In his lifetime* his influence made itself felt only on small groups and among the nondescript multitude. The Pharisees, the Roman centurion, a few friends and adversaries were deeply affected. "And they were astonished at his doctrine; for he taught them as one that had authority, and not as the scribes." But at the same time he was disappointed in the results of his preaching.

To whom did Jesus speak? Essentially, to every man who came his way. What mattered was the inner illumination that enabled the believer to see and love. But he leaned chiefly toward the poor, the outcasts, the sinners, because their souls are shaken and therefore ready for the new faith. "They that are whole have no need of the physician, but they that are sick; I came not to call the righteous, but sinners." "The publicans and the harlots go into the kingdom of God before you." Furthest from him were men who feel sheltered and secure, those fettered to possessions in this world: "A rich man shall hardly enter into the kingdom of heaven." Not the smug Pharisee who prays: "God, I thank thee, that I am not as other men are, extortioners, unjust, adulterers, or even as this publican," will find peace in God, but rather the publican who dared not so much as lift up his eyes unto heaven, but smote upon his breast, saying: "God, be merciful to me, a sinner." The parable of the prodigal son makes his attitude very clear.

Jesus did not content himself with random contacts on his wanderings. He sent out the apostles as "fishers of men," to announce the impending end of the world and the coming of the kingdom. He sent them forth by two and two, "and commanded them that they should take nothing for their journey, save a staff only; no scrip, no bread, no money in their purse; but be shod with sandals; and put on two coats."

The area of their preaching is restricted: "Go not into the way of the Gentiles, . . . but go rather to the lost sheep of the house of Israel." For the world would end even before they had "gone over the cities of Israel."

Jesus learned to his sorrow how paltry and unreliable the results of his preaching could be. The seed falls on fertile and on barren soil. Many receive the message with joy, but they are children of the moment. The cares of the world, the delusion of riches, carnal desires stifle the word. Nearly all have a pretext, like the wedding guests in the parable. Jesus utters his disappointment. "I stood in the midst of the world . . . and found all men drunken, and none did I find thirsting among them, and my soul is afflicted for the sons of men, because they are blind in their heart and see not." "Many are called but few are chosen."

B. While Jesus lived, the disciples shared his belief in God, in the kingdom of heaven, and the end of the world. *When he died,* they dispersed. But soon they regathered and a revolutionary event had occurred. They had seen Jesus risen from the dead. Now they no longer believed with Jesus in God, but without Jesus in Christ arisen. The step had been taken from the religion proclaimed by Jesus the man, a prophet of the Jewish religion, to the Christian religion. While Jesus lived, there was no such thing. How the step was taken, we do not know. "After the death of Jesus, the first Christians withdrew from the area of historic perception, for the supporters of Christ became an utterly intangible thing, oscillating ambiguously between being and nonbeing. It was Paul who first led Christianity into the sphere of history. It is a delusion to make Christianity begin with Jesus as a historical individual" (Overbeck).

Only the direct impact of his personality on those who were close to him can explain how the disciples, in their first bewilderment after his death, arrived at their grandiose interpretation of the crucifixion, which was the beginning of Christianity. But what is Christianity?

The history of Christianity is not yet complete. Because of the part played by the Church in remaking a Western world that had fallen into barbarism, and because the entire spiritual life of Latin and Germanic Europe is permeated with motifs originating in Christianity, all Christian churches seem to have something in common. This common element forms a bond between the many Christian churches that have fought each other to the death, the orthodox and the heretics, and even the indifferent who have grown up in the Christian world. But it is not permissible to define the common element as the "essence" of Christianity and on the basis of such a definition to judge what is Christian and what is not. From a historical point of view, such definitions can never be anything more than speculative ideal types of Christianity or dogmatic tenets on the strength of which particular churches or groups claim to be the sole repositories of Christianity, while all others are no better than heretics or heathen. Thus, insofar as the Western world is Christian, this Christian element, when it is not usurped by limited groups from the Roman Catholic Church to the Protestant sects, can only be the Biblical religion, which encompasses all Christian faiths as well as the Jews and those who believe without a church, and even in some way those who expressly abjure all faith. Biblical religion thus becomes the all-embracing whole, reaching through the millennia from Abraham to our own day; no Westerner can disregard it, but no one is entitled to claim it for his own possession. Every man who lives in a bond with the Biblical religion finds his sustenance in it, selecting and stressing what he wishes. It is only when all the figures of the Biblical religion have been forgotten that the Christian West will be at an end.

Jesus is one element in the Biblical religion, an element of paramount importance for those who believe him to be the Christ. Yet though Jesus Christ is the beginning and center of this creed, Jesus himself, even in the Christian world, is only a component of Christianity; he was not its founder and through him alone it would not have come into being. The reality of Jesus was overlaid by ideas that were alien to him. He was made into something different, but a vestige of his own reality has always remained.

His influence can be summarized along two separate lines: 1. He was transformed from Jesus to Christ, the Son of God, from a human reality to an object of faith. 2. The man himself was taken as a model.

1. His disciples took a first step when they began to believe not only in his message but also in him. Subsequently, they came to believe in him as the Messiah, as the Son of God, as God Himself. With this the human reality became irrelevant, except for two points: that he had actually lived in the flesh and that he had been crucified. It is characteristic that in the Credo the human reality of Jesus disappears. Its second article is a profession of faith in God's only-begotten Son, our Lord, conceived of the Holy Ghost and born of the Virgin Mary. After this transcendent introduction nothing is said of his life except that he suffered under Pontius Pilate, that he was crucified, died, and was buried. After that, we return to the transcendent: he descends to hell, rises from the dead on the third day, ascends to heaven, sits at God's right hand, whence he will come again to judge the living and the dead.

Kierkegaard drew the consequence. All that matters is that God was in the world and was crucified. The historical reality is irrelevant for faith. The study of the New Testament is superfluous for faith, and disturbing. For faith is not based on a historical reality that can be ascertained by critical investigation. Even the faith of his contemporaries, who saw Jesus in the flesh, who knew his life, his gestures, actions, words, was not a product of the reality.

This belief in the Christ was not inaugurated by Jesus but sprang up after his death. The first step was belief in the resurrection, based on the visions of Mary Magdalene and several of the apostles. Next, the shameful death on the cross was transformed into an act of sacrifice. Finally, with the out-pouring of the Holy Ghost, the meaning of the company of believers was actualized and became the Church. The Gospel narrative of the Last Supper became the basis of a cult. The sacrament of the Last Supper was the end of a development; had Jesus established it, it would necessarily have been the beginning. "Jesus did not make himself into a sacrament" (von Soden).

The articles of faith: Christ's sacrificial death; the redemption of all be-lievers through this death, wherein Christ took their sins upon himself; justification by faith; Christ as the second Person in the Trinity; Christ as Logos (world reason), participating in the creation of the world and guiding the people of Israel through the desert; the Church as Christ's *corpus mysticum;* Christ as the second Adam, historical beginning of a new man-kind; all these tenets and many more that mark the rich history of Christian dogma have nothing to do with Jesus. Christ was a new reality that was to produce the most overwhelming effects in history.

2. Without the churches, Christianity could not have developed through the centuries. If Jesus kept a place amid the innumerable motifs that entered into this development, it was thanks to the canon of the Christian Scriptures. While even so early a Christian as Paul had no interest in Jesus the man, the Gospels remained a part of the New Testament. The Christian canon, including the books of the Old Testament, is so rich in contradictory themes that there is no justification for trying to find anywhere in it the key to the Gospel, to the message of Jesus, to the Biblical religion. Even Jesus is not the key. But it was his reality that gave the impetus wherever the idea of the imitation of Jesus has arisen.

Here and there, men have taken a radical view of "imitation." They have tried to put the Sermon on the Mount into practice by turning the other cheek, to follow Jesus' instructions to the apostles by wandering in poverty, to follow the Passion by provoking their own ruin in the world, in short, to achieve the truth of martyrdom by actively imitating Jesus' most extreme actions and sayings.

Or else, the imitation of Jesus has been interpreted as the transfiguration of the suffering that comes to us unsummoned, in the course of events. The Passion of Jesus becomes a model, teaching us to bear the most unjust and inexplicable suffering, not to despair when we are forsaken, to find God, the last and only foothold, at the source of all things, to bear our cross with patience. For all suffering is sanctified through Jesus.

The imitation of Jesus takes on still another meaning when his ethical imperatives are taken as a norm, when purity and love are seen as God's will. This attitude compels knowledge: even at best we experience our ethical inadequacy.

But an orientation by Jesus is possible without imitation. For Jesus gave the example of a life whose meaning was not nullified by failure in the world, but enhanced, not to be sure as an unequivocal directive but as a manifest possibility. He showed how a man could become free from the fear inherent in life by taking his cross upon himself. His message teaches men to keep their eyes open for absolute evil in the world and forbids complacency; it reminds men of the existence of a higher authority. The absurdities in his words and actions can exert a liberating effect.

Many men in the world of Biblical religion have managed to discern Jesus through all the successive layers of tradition. In his actions and words he spoke as himself. Because of his radicalism, which has never ceased to be meaningful, the contemplation of Jesus the man has always been a source of inspiration. He has remained a powerful force in opposition to the Christianity that made him into its foundation, the dynamite which has threatened so often to shatter the congealed, worldly Christianity of the churches. He is invoked by the heretics who take their radicalism seriously.

Enormous intellectual efforts have been made to confine the contradictory flow of this man's life and thought in a systematic whole. In their drive toward worldly order, the churches have tried, often with considerable success, to muffle his explosive power, to limit and direct the flame. But from time to time it has broken loose, bringing new hopes and fears of the catastrophe that would usher in the kingdom of heaven.

This origin has created peculiar difficulties for Church dogma and policy, and these never-resolved difficulties in turn have been responsible for the lack of clarity, but also for the vitality and wonderful truthfulness of Christianity.

The difficulty began when the world failed to end. In the new situation, thought and action had to be revised. In practice, the place of the expected kingdom was taken by the Church. Jesus, the herald of the end, became the institutor of the sacrament. But once the kingdom of God that would end history was drawn into history, its whole character inevitably changed. The application of a message springing from the most extreme of situations to the tasks of this world, to the shaping of existence, the promotion of knowledge, art, letters, gave rise to the insoluble antinomies that mark any discussion of "Christianity and Culture." Rebels and dogmatists have formed equally rigid and narrow conceptions of Jesus, the man and his teaching. The rebels' interests lead them to seek grounds on which to deny everything in the world, as justification for their destructive drive for power. The advocates of Church dogma are led by their interests to moderate what is explosive and extreme by finding a place for it within the eternal, unchanging truth of Christianity. Thus they cannot acknowledge that the failure of the world to end produced a revision of Christian thinking.

In regard to the historic knowledge of Jesus, orthodox faith may favor a radical skepticism which makes it possible to fill in the empty space, where the historic reality had been, with a life of Christ based solely on faith and immune to historical criticism because it is not empirical but transcendent. Or, on the contrary, it may recognize the whole Gospel narrative as a historic reality to be believed without critical investigation. In the first case, historical knowledge is quite logically eschewed as irrelevant to faith. In the second, critical investigation is limited to secondary matters, for it is not permitted to alter so much as a jot in the revealed, absolutely certain empirical reality of the Biblical accounts.

The historic reality of Jesus, the man, which is so extremely important for us in the history of philosophy, is without interest to the doctors of the faith, either among the rebels or the orthodox believers.

1. WHY THESE FOUR?

We might have considered others: Abraham, Moses, Elijah, Zoroaster, Isaiah, Jeremiah, Mohammed, Lao-tzu, Pythagoras. But none of these had a historical influence of equal breadth and duration. Only one, Mohammed, might be comparable in historical importance but not in individual depth.

To the inquirer all four present the same methodological situation. All the texts by which we know them came into being after their death. Philological and historical criticism shows the original figures to be overlaid by legends and myths which not infrequently may be traced to sources in no way related to them. Critical study of the texts sometimes yields relative certainties, but more often we must content ourselves with probabilities and for the most part with mere possibilities.

The findings of historical criticism cannot be ignored, but they cannot produce a picture of the historical reality. For when we sift out the historical certainties, the result is a very scant minimum. When we strip off the accumulated layers of tradition to arrive at the original reality of the great men, it evades us. There simply are no reliable historical accounts. Almost every point in the tradition is subject to historical doubt. In the end it becomes possible to doubt these men's very existence (as has actually happened in connection with Buddha and Jesus), because it seems to vanish completely behind myth and legend. The absurdity of such a conclusion suggests doubts in the methods of criticism itself.

The historical reality of these great men can be discerned only in their extraordinary impact on those who knew them and in its later echoes. This impact is demonstrable. Pictures of these men were conceived from the very beginning and recorded by writers who regarded themselves as followers. Such images are themselves a historical reality.

The people of every epoch have seen these images of the paradigmatic individuals as a reality and this is what we must do today, but under new conditions. Critical analyses of the traditions have prepared us to see beyond the documents. In studying the sources, we let the image take form within us. Like the men of all other periods, we may look at the reality directly, independently of the defined, fixated faith. Criticism, to be sure, imposes limits on this vision and demands a certain preparation. But, once gained, the vision has all its original freshness. It remains indemonstrable and cannot be arrived at by reasoning. What is seen in this way becomes a guide to criticism; in itself it proves nothing and merely proposes questions concerning which reasoning is possible. Critical doubt joined to a feeling for the tradition cannot but encourage us to risk forming a picture of the historic reality.

Which of the four are best known to us? Our knowledge of Jesus and Socrates would seem to be better substantiated than our knowledge of Buddha. As to the authenticity of the sayings, Buddha's are more open to doubt than those of Socrates, Jesus, and Confucius. But they are all doubtful. Each of the four figures stands out clearly. But the light in which we see them seems to vary. We see Socrates in a realistic daylight; Jesus is transfigured as though by magic; Buddha appears as a type, in an aura of enchanted abstraction; Confucius walks soberly in the bright light of this world. Is Socrates more tangibly present and more coherent because the other three had no Plato? Or are some words of Jesus better authenticated because the apostles were not writers and did not consciously try to produce literature?

Mere criticism ends in the conclusion that we can know nothing definitely. The reality vanishes. And yet we continue to perceive it. This vision can be justified:

These four men were given their high place in tradition before the birth of scientific criticism. Perhaps it was a prejudice to suppose that what for many hundreds of years produced so extraordinary an effect on the inner attitudes of men really existed. But such a prejudice seems to have a good deal in its favor. It is not possible that a man's insignificance will turn to greatness in an image, that other men's picture of an insignificant man will reveal such loftiness of soul. The source of the image must itself have been extraordinary.

In any case we know that these men's influence began at once, in their lifetime, that it first emanated from a living man and not from an image. And we ourselves are caught up in the experience of this indubitable impact. The power it still has over us is not a rational proof, but it is an indication that cannot be ignored. These men are still visible because their influence is still at work.

Criticism leans toward the belief that the source of these men's greatness was not in themselves but rather that, in beginning to crystallize, a social order, a congregation, a church, in any case something outside them, took them as a nucleus around which to deposit all manner of myths and spiritual contents. The original point, it is believed, has disappeared from view, and rightly so, for the beginning is not what mattered.

Our sense of reality rejects such a thesis. Can accident make something enduring out of nothing? In political affairs, perhaps, a man insignificant in himself may be enabled by fortuitous circumstances to produce an important effect and thus gain for a time a considerable outward power. But such a man cannot move the depths of men's souls. His power over men cannot endure.

Criticism also suggests that the great men may be interpreted as types common in their time. Socrates was very much like Simon the Shoemaker or the Sophists; Confucius was one of the itinerant scribes and advisers, Buddha one of many founders of monastic orders, Jesus one of the Jews who claimed to be the Messiah and were executed. The notion is instructive, because it applies to the sociological phenomenon, though not, of course, to the individuality of these men. Any attempt to assimilate them to types helps to bring out their historical uniqueness. Why did Socrates, Buddha, Jesus, Confucius exert so immense an influence, and not the others? What historical criticism leaves of them provides no answer.

How, under the present conditions, shall we proceed to form an image of these great men? It is assumed that we have been moved by their reality. This does not mean that an arbitrary subjectivity is substituted for historical knowledge, but rather that historical knowledge will be used to elucidate an experience without which historic knowledge would be meaningless.

In forming our picture, we must verify the testimony that has come down to us. This may be done according to the following principles: The traditional material is arranged according to subject matter in such a way as to disclose ideal types, convincing by their inner consistency. For each of the great men several of these ideal constructions will take form. We shall compare them, looking for the polarity within the unity. For there is greatness in the range of the contradictions that are held together. So far we have considered the original phenomenon distinct from the deviations and perversions that enter into the tradition from the beginning and become more and more abundant as time goes on. These too should be elucidated. Through them the origin takes on greater clarity, for in it we find the ground of their possibility. And such an investigation helps to refute the false criticism which takes the deviations for the thing itself.

But we must bear in mind that no image can be absolutely valid; and above all, that easy as they are to enunciate, our principles of interpretation can never be fully applied.

2. THE COMMON GROUND AND

THE DIFFERENCES

These men set norms by their attitudes, actions, experience of being, and their imperatives. In delving to the heart of their own problems, subsequent philosophers have looked to these thinkers. Each in his sphere, they have all exerted an enormous influence on later philosophy. In the interest of philosophy we shall here consider briefly what they have in common and how on this common ground they characteristically differ.

A. From the standpoint of *sociology,* we observe that one was descended from the high aristocracy (Buddha), the rest from the common people. None was without roots, each belonged to a society with a well-defined mode of life.

From a *psychological* point of view, their masculine character is striking. They were without family sentiment, although three of them (Socrates, Confucius, Buddha) were married. But they had deep feeling for their students or disciples. Their basic masculine attitude was natural, not a product of will or principle.

B. *They do not conform to the prophet type* characterized by visions and ecstasies. They did not hear or see God directly; they received no direct mission to divulge His definite revealed will. But all are in a way related to the prophets. They know themselves to be in the service of the Godhead, called by God (Socrates, Confucius, Jesus) or as the appointed instrument of a necessary redemption (Buddha). But their message does not spring from direct revelation. Like the prophets, they know loneliness and silence, and illumination through meditation. But they are prophets in a greater sense: in them a chasm has opened. The world is not in order. A radical change is experienced and demanded. They are stirred to their depths, by what we do not know. They express what there is no appropriate way of saying. They speak in parables, dialectical contradictions, conversational replies; they do not fixate. They indicate what is to be done, but in such a way that it cannot be directly understood through any technique of instrumentality, still less as a program for a new world order. They break through the customary, through what had hitherto been taken for granted, and through the merely intelligible. They create new possibilities and a new area populated with beginnings that are never carried to completion.

C. *"Transformation":* The essential is not their work or its content, but a living reality that was the beginning of a human transformation in the world. The demands they make on us are never fully expressed in instructions that need merely be followed. In order to understand them, one must experience some sort of transformation, a rebirth, a new awareness of reality, an illumination. The transformation exacted by Socrates is a transformation in thinking; Buddha calls for meditation and the way of life that goes with it, Confucius for a process of education that is more than mere learning, Jesus for a devotion to God's will that rules out the world.

D. *Death and suffering:* Socrates and Jesus suffered death at the hands of the worldly powers; Buddha was started on his career by the reality of death; Confucius saw death but gave it no weight. In each case we find a characteristic relation to these basic elements of human existence, death, and suffering.

Socrates died in peace at the age of seventy, his serenity clouded neither by exaltation nor by any vestige of vital anguish. He had the composure of one who knows how to die. Granted a gentle death by hemlock poisoning, he died without the pathos of martyrdom. Yet without this death he might not have become the Socrates who has stirred men ever since; the disciples and Plato might not have seen the figure whose greatness, in the profound emotion of the days before his death, appeared to them in the recasting of their own hearts and continued to grow in their memory.

Jesus died on the cross, a young man of thirty. He died the most cruel and degrading of deaths, and through him all the terror and anguish of violent death are brought home to us. He rebelled against his death and took it upon himself as God's will. Without this death Jesus would not have become the Christ, he would not have arisen and become an object of faith.

By the challenge of their death and the manner of their dying, Socrates and Jesus are answers to the question of death. In them the Western world has recognized two mirrors of itself: in Socrates the serene peace of mind that attaches no importance to death—in Jesus an attitude which finds the ground of transcendence in extreme affliction and in torment surpassing human endurance.

These historic figures—Socrates and Jesus—grew to the stature of mythical archetypes. In their concrete humanity men came to see what they had seen in mythical figures such as Gilgamesh and Job, the suffering servant of God in Deutero-Isaiah, the heroes of Greek tragedy. The universal themes of myth—existence is suffering, activity is the conquest of suffering, but all great activity is doomed to failure—were embodied in Socrates and Jesus. Beyond all others, these two have stirred and exalted men, Socrates as the philosopher who fails in the world, Jesus as the man whose life in the world is an impossibility, whose only bond is with God.

Our usual condition is one of heartless unfeeling. The most frightful things can happen around us, the most hideous wrongs can be inflicted on men by men—we are seized with pity and no doubt with apprehension that such things may happen to us, but then we are caught up again in the business of existence, and in the main we forget and muffle our compassion. In regard to those who are anonymous and far away, we are not even touched by compassion.

This was not the way of the paradigmatic individuals. They were not afflicted with the lack of imagination of our average man. To Buddha and Jesus, suffering and death were the true reality of this worldly existence, and it was this reality that they conquered by their life, vision, and thought. They expressed this experience in terms of the inconceivable: only Nirvana and the kingdom of heaven are eternal. Socrates and Confucius looked death so straight in the eye that it lost its significance.

E. *Love your enemies:* For all of them human love was universal and unlimited. All asked the ultimate question: How shall I act toward my enemy
who wrongs me? But their answers were not identical. The radical injunction to love our enemies occurs only in Jesus. Lao-tzu also bids men answer
enmity with benevolence. But Confucius rejects this imperative and declares:
"Requite kindness with kindness, enmity with justice." Socrates says in the
Crito: "Doing evil in retaliation for evil is not just." And "Neither injury
nor retaliation nor warding off evil by evil is ever right." He knows the
demand is extraordinary: "For this opinion has never been held . . . and
those who are agreed and those who are not agreed upon this point have
not common ground, and can only despise one another" (but in Xenophon
he takes a different point of view). Buddha teaches the universal love
which offers no resistance to the evildoer, suffers with infinite patience,
and does good to all living things.

F. *The question of how to overcome suffering and death is at the same time
the question of our relation to the world.* By thinking in the world Socrates
seeks himself and his relation to other men. By his extreme questioning
he arouses a real, living certainty that is not mere knowledge of something.
He transcends the world without negating it. He forgoes total knowledge,
total judgments, contenting himself with a nonknowledge in which truth
and reality are actualized.

His way is so difficult because by nature men seek to know definitely
and tangibly what is; they seek objective precepts.

Buddha strives by contemplation and a life free from the world to
attain Nirvana and leave the world. His suffering, which was a participation in the sufferings of all creatures, was boundless. He believed he had
found liberation: the dissolution of existence in the whole, not by violent
destruction, which would only have led to new existence, but by a transcending wherein its drives are extinguished. This is the way of nonviolent
renunciation in the stillness of the soul.

The limitation of Buddha's insight is that it limits experience and hence
ignores all the spiritual contents which the mind can acquire only by entering into the world. This limits his compassion, for he has eyes only for a
small range of human sufferings, scarcely exceeding those inherent in the
life process. Thus there is no development of man's nature through the
fulfillment of the world, through the shaping of experience in the world.
All essential knowledge is already attained and the possibilities of life in
the world are lost by indifference.

Confucius wishes to help man to mold himself in his world and enable
the world to shape itself in its foreordained eternal order. He strives for the
fulfillment of man, through the idea of natural humanity under the conditions prevailing in the world. He regards this as possible because the world
itself is subject to the prototype of the *tao* and is not merely guided by expedience and practical utility.

His limitation, which explains the insuccess of his world idea, is that in the face of evil and failure he merely laments and suffers with dignity, but derives no impulsion from the abyss.

With unlimited radicalism, Jesus breaks through all worldly orders. Without denying the world, he subjects all things to the condition of the kingdom that will come at the end of the world; in this light he assays their eternal value as good or evil, true or false. In rebellion looking to the end of the world, Jesus established an unconditional ethos in harmony with God's will.

His limitation is that in this vision there could be no place for building in the world.

Socrates founded no school or other institution; his communication with men was free and unplanned. Buddha inaugurated a monastic community that would open the way to Nirvana to its members by attaining an absolute ethos; but since in practice the monks who had achieved the goal could be expected to go on living for a while, they would carry the liberating knowledge to all accessible men. Confucius founded a school whereby to guide the world back to its proper order by giving it statesmen with an ethical cast of mind. Jesus proclaimed, and bade his apostles proclaim, the end of the world and the coming of the kingdom of heaven.

All wished to transcend the world, either by leaving it behind, or by putting order into its anarchy. All were governed by a transcendent power. Their conduct in the world, their way of combating evil—even when it consisted in a striving to order the world—reaches out beyond human plans and endeavors, because it is guided by a higher authority.

Schematically, we may say that Socrates, in the world, goes the way of thought, of human reason; this is the way that distinguishes man, his characteristic potentiality. Buddha strives to annul the world by extinguishing the will to existence. Confucius aspires to build a world. Jesus is the world's crisis.

G. *Modes of communication:* All four communicate their thought and take it as their mission to do so.

In the streets and on the highroads, they move among men, speaking with them, exchanging questions and answers, expounding their doctrines, which they modified according to the situation.

Their concern was not mere knowledge, but a transformation in men's thinking and inward action. But how does one reach the innermost soul of other men? The answer of the four to this question is not theoretical but practical. All four knew that they were speaking to the profound inwardness that precedes all action. And they knew their message to be grounded in an absolute which may be called being, eternity, God, or an order manifested in the archetypes, but which ceases to be its own authentic self once it is considered thus objectively.

Who is accessible to such doctrines? Buddha replies: "The doctrine belongs to the man of understanding, not to the fool." But Jesus answers: "Let the little children come unto me." Socrates differentiates, his daimonion objects when unsuitable persons seek association with him. Confucius takes talent into consideration. Jesus addresses all men.

Let us compare Jesus and Buddha: Jesus' message is part of a history wrought by God. Those who go with Jesus are caught up in a passion that has its source in the moment of the most critical decision. Buddha proclaims his doctrine in aimless wanderings, in aristocratic serenity, without insistence, indifferent to a world that is forever the same. Jesus builds on the Old Testament, Buddha on Hindu philosophy. Jesus demands faith, Buddha demands insight.

Let us compare Jesus with Socrates: Jesus teaches by proclaiming the glad tidings, Socrates by compelling men to think. Jesus demands faith, Socrates an exchange of thought. Jesus speaks with direct earnestness, Socrates indirectly, even by irony. Jesus knows of the kingdom of heaven and eternal life, Socrates has no definite knowledge of these matters and leaves the question open. But neither will let men rest. Jesus proclaims the only way; Socrates leaves man free, but keeps reminding him of his responsibility rooted in freedom. Both raise supreme claims. Jesus confers salvation. Socrates provokes men to look for it.

H. *Silence and nonknowledge:* All four know silence and lay stress on it. They conceal nothing, but their profoundest truth can be communicated only indirectly even to themselves. They speak in parables, fall silent at certain times, expressly decline to answer questions they regard as inappropriate. None of them is interested in metaphysical speculation or the science of nature. There are large realms that they have no desire to know.

All come to a point where they insist on their nonknowledge. Where knowledge is not attainable, time should not be wasted on fruitless pondering. Even in great questions knowledge is not necessary unless the salvation of the soul depends on it. The many traditional orders and modes of life are sufficient in the world; it is just as well to observe them if they do not come into conflict with the fundamental aim.

3. OUR ATTITUDE TOWARD
THE FOUR PARADIGMATIC INDIVIDUALS

They are not philosophers, insofar as science was a matter of indifference to them and philosophy is thinking along the pathways of science, which it presupposes. They do not take their place in the history of philosophy with any rational positions. They wrote no works. Three of them are regarded by large religious communities as their founders. In what sense then are they to be claimed for philosophy?

Religion in the sense of Church ritual and dogma is not essential to their being. They are a historical reality that makes demands on philosophy and organized religion alike and rejects any claim to exclusive ownership by either philosophy or religion. Philosophy may merely claim the right to derive inspiration from the experience of these great men and from their personal reality.

Originality and a life at their own risk, without any pre-existing community to support their actions—these are common to all four. All four became models for mankind without setting themselves up as examples (the "I am the way, the truth, and the life" of the Gospel of St. John was surely not spoken by Jesus). But they became models; though the immensity of their being could never be adequately stated in law and idea, they set their stamp on humanity. And it was only then that men transformed their images to the point of deification.

For philosophy they are men. As men they must have their particular traits of character, their limitations; because they are historical, they cannot have universal validity for all. There are four of them; no one can be taken exclusively and alone. Where one of them is absolutized as the one and only truth, it means that believers have divested his image of all natural humanity.

The core of their reality is an experience of the fundamental human situation and a discovery of the human task. They speak to us of these things. In so doing they arrive at extreme questions to which they give answers. All of them fulfilled ultimate human potentialities. This is their common ground, but it does not make them one. Nor can they be combined into a synthesis of the truth. They are related because they lived and inquired and answered on the basis of human possibilities, but they are also distinct individuals. They cannot be pieced together to form a single man who might travel all their ways at once.

But this they have in common: in them human experiences and aspirations are manifested in the extreme. What was essential in them will always be essential for philosophy. Their reality and modes of thought are an essential element in our history. They became sources of philosophical thought and a stimulus to resistance, through whom the resisters first gained self-awareness.

Our philosophical attitude toward them is this: We are moved by what they have in common, because we stand with them in the situation of being men. None of them can be indifferent to us. Each one is a question addressed to us that leaves us no peace.

We become aware that in our own reality we follow none of them. Once the distance between our own questionable lives and the earnestness of these great men is brought home to us, we feel impelled to summon up all the earnestness of which we are capable. Herein they are beacons by which to gain an orientation, not models to imitate.

Each of the four has his own greatness, an area in which he is not comparable with the others. Socrates and Confucius point to pathways that we too can travel, though not as they did. In general, the contents of their thinking cannot be ours. But the manner of their thinking can show us the way. As for Jesus and Buddha, not only the content, but also the forms of life and thought are closed to us—or else we must make a decision and draw the consequences without which everything remains a pretense.

I believe that nearly all Westerners who look at the matter impartially will agree with this estimate. Only the neglect of crucial points or interpretations that becloud certain essentials can lead the average Westerner to suppose that he is seriously imitating Jesus, not to mention Buddha. Such hypocrisies have nothing to do with the possibility of a true imitation. Where it actually occurs, it commands respect. But one who philosophizes should clearly see the conditions under which such imitation is possible and the inescapable consequences. Only then can he know, in the concrete situations of his life, what he is doing and what he wants.

BIBLIOGRAPHY

EDITOR'S NOTE

The Bibliography is based on that given in the German original. English translations are given wherever possible. Selected English and American works have been added; these are marked by an asterisk.

Socrates

SOURCES:

The Dialogues of Plato, trans. by Benjamin Jowett. 2 vols. New York, Random House, 1937.

Plato: *The Dialogues,* trans. by Floyer Sydenham and Thomas Taylor. 5 vols. London, printed for Thomas Taylor by R. Wilks, 1804.

Plato's dialogues (in roughly chronological order, no certain sequence having been established. English translations other than those listed above are given).

Ion.

Hippias Minor.

Hippias Maior (?).

Protagoras, Benjamin Jowett's trans., rev. by Martin Ostwald, ed. by G. Vlastos. New York, Liberal Arts Press, 1956.

Apology, in *Euthyphro, Apology, Crito and Symposium,* Benjamin Jowett's trans., rev. by Moses Hadas. Chicago, H. Regnery Co., 1953.

Crito, in *Euthyphro, Apology, Crito and Symposium,* Benjamin Jowett's trans., rev. by Moses Hadas. Chicago, H. Regnery Co., 1953.

Laches.

Charmides.

Euthyphro, in *Euthyphro, Apology, Crito and Symposium,* Benjamin Jowett's trans., rev. by Moses Hadas. Chicago, H. Regnery Co., 1953.

Lysis.

Gorgias.

Menexenos.

Meno, in *Protagoras and Meno,* trans. by W. K. C. Guthrie. (Penguin Classics.) Harmondsworth, Penguin Books, 1956.

Euthydemus.

Cratylus.

Phaedo, trans. with introduction and commentary by Reginald Hackforth. Cambridge, Cambridge University Press, 1955.

Symposium, trans. by Walter Hamilton. (Penguin Classics.) London and Baltimore, Penguin Books, 1952.

The Republic, trans. by Francis Macdonald Cornford. New York, Oxford University Press, 1956.

Phaedrus, trans. by Reginald Hackforth. Cambridge, Cambridge University Press, 1952.

Parmenides, in *Plato and Parmenides: Parmenides' Way of Truth and Plato's Parmenides,* trans. with introduction and running commentary by Francis Macdonald Cornford. New York, Liberal Arts Press, 1957.

Theaetetus, in *Plato's Theory of Knowledge: the Theaetetus and the Sophist of Plato,* trans. with running commentary by Francis Macdonald Cornford. (Liberal Arts Library.) London, Routledge and Kegan Paul, 1951.

Sophist, in *Plato's Theory of Knowledge: the Theaetetus and the Sophist of Plato,* trans. with running commentary by Francis Macdonald Cornford. (Liberal Arts Library.) London, Routledge and Kegan Paul, 1951.

Statesman, trans. of *Politicus* by Joseph Bright Skemp. New Haven, Yale University Press, 1952.

Philebus, in *Philebus and Epinomis,* trans. by Alfred Edward Taylor. New York, Thomas Nelson & Sons, 1956.

Timaeus, in *Plato's Cosmology: the Timaeus of Plato,* trans. with running commentary by Francis Macdonald Cornford. New York, Humanities Press, 1957. *Critias.*

The Laws, trans. by Alfred Edward Taylor. London, Dent, 1934.

Xenophon: *Memorabilia* and *Oeconomicus,* trans. by E. C. Marchant. (Loeb Classical Library.) Cambridge, Mass., Harvard University Press; London, Wm. Heinemann, Ltd., 1923.

——: *Apology and Symposium,* trans. by O. J. Todd. (Loeb Classical Library.) London, Wm. Heinemann, Ltd.; New York, G. P. Putnam's Sons, 1927.

Aristophanes: *The Clouds,* trans. anonymous. In Vol. II of *The Complete Greek Drama,* ed. by Whitney J. Oates and Eugene O'Neill, Jr. 2 vols. New York, Random House, 1938.

Aristotle: *Metaphysics,* Book I, ch. 6; Book XIII, ch. 4. In *The Basic Works of Aristotle,* ed. by Richard McKeon. New York, Random House, 1941.

SECONDARY WORKS:

Bruns, Ivo: *Das literarische Portrait der Griechen im fünften und vierten Jahrhundert vor Christi Geburt.* Berlin, Wilhelm Hertz, 1896.

*Burnet, John: *Greek Philosophy, Part I: Thales to Plato.* London, Macmillan, 1914.

*Cornford, Francis Macdonald: *Principium Sapientiae: the Origins of Greek Philosophical Thought,* ed. by W. K. C. Guthrie, ch. 5. Cambridge, Cambridge University Press, 1952.

*——: *Before and after Socrates.* Cambridge, Cambridge University Press, 1932.

Gigon, Olof: *Socrates—Sein Bild in Dichtung und Geschichte.* Berne, Francke, 1947.

Guardini, Romano: *The Death of Socrates, an Interpretation of the Platonic Dialogues: Euthyphro, Apology, Crito, and Phaedo,* trans. by Basil Wrighton. London, Sheed, 1948.

Jaeger, Werner Wilhelm: *Paideia: the Ideals of Greek Culture,* trans. by Gilbert Highet, Vol. II. New York, Oxford University Press, 1943.

Maier, Heinrich: *Sokrates—Sein Werk und seine geschichtliche Stellung.* Tübingen, J. C. B. Mohr, 1913.

Meyer, Eduard: *Geschichte des Altertums,* Vol. IV², pp. 150-75; Vol. V, pp. 207 ff. 5 vols. in 8. Basel, B. Schwabe, 1953-58.

Stenzel, Julius: "Sokrates," in Pauly-Wissowa, *Realencyclopädie.* Stuttgart, J. B. Metzler, 1929.

——: *Plato's Method of Dialectic.* Oxford, Clarendon Press, 1940.
Taylor, Alfred Edward: *Socrates.* Boston, Beacon Press, 1951.

Buddha

SOURCES:

The Buddhist (Pali) Canon:
Dialogues of the Buddha [*Dīgha-Nikāya*]. Trans. by T. W. and C. A. F. Rhys
 Davids (Sacred Books of the Buddhists, Vols. 2, 3, 4). 3 vols. London, Oxford
 University Press, 1899-1921.
Further Dialogues of the Buddha [*Majjhima-Nikāya*]. Trans. by Lord Chalmers
 (Sacred Books of the Buddhists, Vols. 5, 6). 2 vols. London, Oxford University
 Press, 1926-7.
The Book of the Kindred Sayings [*Samyutta-Nikāya*]. Trans. by C. A. F. Rhys
 Davids and F. L. Woodward. 5 vols. London, Oxford University Press (for Pali
 Text Society), 1917-30.
The Book of the Gradual Sayings [*Anguttara-Nikāya*]. Trans. by F. L. Woodward
 and E. M. Hare. 5 vols. London, Luzac and Co. (for Pali Text Society), 1932-6.
The Minor Anthologies of the Pali Canon. Trans. by C. A. F. Rhys Davids, F. L.
 Woodward, *et al.* 4 vols. London, Oxford University Press and Luzac and Co.
 (for Pali Text Society), 1931-42. (Includes *Dhammapada, Khuddaka-Patha,
 Udana,* etc.)
Psalms of the Brethren. Psalms of the Sisters [*Thera Theri-Gāthā*]. Translated by
 C. A. F. Rhys Davids. 2 vols. London, Oxford University Press, 1909.
Buddhist Suttas. Translated by T. W. Rhys Davids. (Sacred Books of the East,
 Vol. 11,) Oxford, Clarendon Press, 1881.
Dhammapada. Trans. and ed. by S. Radhakrishnan. London, Oxford University
 Press, 1950.

SELECTIONS FROM THE SOURCES, IN TRANSLATION:
Buddhism in Translations. Ed. by Henry Clarke Warren. (Harvard Oriental Series,
 Vol. 3.) Cambridge, Mass., Harvard University Press, 1896.
Early Buddhist Scriptures. Trans. and ed. by E. J. Thomas. London, Kegan Paul,
 1935.
Buddhist Texts through the Ages. Ed. by Edward Conze. Oxford, Bruno Cassirer,
 1954.
The Teachings of the Compassionate Buddha. Ed. by E. A. Burtt. New York,
 Mentor Books, 1955.
Buddhist Scriptures. Selected and edited by Edward Conze. Harmondsworth and
 Baltimore, Penguin Books, 1959.
The Vedāntic Buddhism of the Buddha. A Collection of Historical Texts. Trans-
 lated and edited by J. G. Jennings. London, Oxford University Press, 1947.

SECONDARY WORKS:
*Davids, C. A. F. Rhys: *Gotama the Man.* London, Luzac, 1928.
——: *Sakya, or Buddhist Origins.* London, Kegan Paul, 1931.
*Dutt, Sukumar: *Early Buddhist Monachism, 600 B.C.—100 B.C.* London, Kegan
 Paul; New York, Dutton, 1924.
*Eliot, Sir Charles: *Hinduism and Buddhism.* 3 vols. London, Edward Arnold, 1921.

———: *Japanese Buddhism.* London, Edward Arnold, 1935.

Hackmann, Heinrich: *Buddhism as a Religion.* London, Probsthain, 1910.

———: *Der Buddhismus.* 3 vols. Halle, Gebauer-Schwetschke, 1906.

*Keith, A. B.: *Buddhist Philosophy in India and Ceylon.* London, Oxford University Press, 1923.

Kern, J. Heinrich C.: *Manual of Indian Buddhism.* Strassburg, Trübner, 1896.

Köppen, C. Friedrich: *Die Religion des Buddha.* 2 vols. Berlin, F. Schneider, 1857-9.

*McGovern, W. M.: *A Manual of Buddhist Philosophy.* London, Kegan Paul; New York, Dutton, 1923.

Oldenberg, Hermann: *Buddha: His Life, His Doctrine, His Order.* Trans. by William Hoey. Calcutta, Book Company, 1927.

Pischel, Richard: *Leben und Lehre des Buddha.* 3d ed. Leipzig, Teubner, 1916.

*Poussin, L. de la Vallée: *The Way to Nirvana.* London, Cambridge University Press, 1917.

*Radhakrishnan, Sarvepalli: *Indian Philosophy,* 2d ed. 2 vols. London, Allen and Unwin; New York, Macmillan Co., 1929-31.

Stcherbatsky, Theodore Ippolitovich: *La Théorie de la connaissance et la logique chez les Bouddhistes tardifs.* Trans. by I. de Manziarly and P. Masson-Oursel. Paris, Geuthner, 1926.

*Suzuki, Daisetz Teitaro: *Outlines of Mahayana Buddhism.* London, Luzac, 1907.

*Thomas, E. J.: *The History of Buddhist Thought.* London, Kegan Paul; New York, Knopf, 1933.

———: *The Life of Buddha as Legend and History.* 2d ed. London, Kegan Paul; New York, Knopf, 1931.

Confucius

SOURCES:

The Chinese Canon:

The Five Canonical Books: *Shu King (Shu Ching), Book of History; Shi King (Shih Ching), Book of Odes; I King (I Ching, Yi King), Book of Changes; Li Ki, Record of Rites; Shun Chiu (Ch'un Ts'iu), Spring and Autumn Annals.*

The Confucian Writings: *Ta Hsüeh (Ta Hio), Great Learning; Chung Yung, Doctrine of the Mean; Lun Yü, Analects.*

The Works of Mencius (Meng-tse).

The Texts of Confucianism. Translated by James Legge. 4 vols. (Vol. 1, *Shi King, Hsiao King;* Vol. 2, *I King;* Vols. 3, 4, *Li Ki*). (Sacred Books of the East, Vols. 3, 16, 27, 28.) Oxford, Clarendon Press, 1879-85.

The Chinese Classics. With a translation by James Legge. 5 vols. (Vol. 1, *Analects, Great Learning, Doctrine of the Mean;* Vol. 2, *Works of Mencius;* Vol. 3, *Shu King;* Vol. 4, *Shi [She] King;* Vol. 5. *Shun Chiu [Ch'un-Ts'iu]*). Hongkong, 1861-72.

The I Ching, or Book of Changes. With a foreword by C. G. Jung. The Richard Wilhelm [German] translation, rendered into English by Cary F. Baynes. 2 vols. London, Routledge and Kegan Paul; New York, Pantheon Books (Bollingen Series XIX), 1950, 1951.

The Analects of Confucius. Translated and annotated by Arthur Waley. London, Allen and Unwin, 1938.

The Shu King. Translated by Walter Gorn Old. London and Benares, Theosophical Publishing Society; New York, John Lane, 1904.
The Great Learning and The Mean in Action. Translated by E. R. Hughes. London, Dent, 1942.

SECONDARY WORKS:

*Creel, Herrlea Glessner: *Chinese Thought from Confucius to Mao Tsê-tung.* Chicago, University of Chicago Press; London, Eyre and Spottiswoode, 1953, 1954.
———: *Confucius: The Man and the Myth.* New York, J. Day Co., 1949; London, Routledge and Kegan Paul, 1951.
Crow, Herbert Carl: *Master Kung: The Story of Confucius.* London, Hamish Hamilton, 1937; New York, Harper, 1938.
Forke, Alfred: *Geschichte der alten chinesischen Philosophie.* Hamburg, Friedrichsen, de Gruyter, 1927.
———: *Geschichte der mittelalterlichen chinesischen Philosophie.* Hamburg, Friederichsen, de Gruyter, 1934.
———: *Geschichte der neueren chinesischen Philosophie.* Hamburg, Friederichsen, de Gruyter, 1938.
Franke, O.: *Geschichte des chinesischen Reiches.* 5 vols. Berlin, De Gruyter, 1930-52.
*Fung Yu-lan: *A History of Chinese Philosophy.* Translated by Derk Bodde. 2 vols. Princeton, Princeton University Press, 1952-3; London, Allen and Unwin, 1953.
Gabelentz, Georg von der: *Confucius und seine Lehre.* Leipzig, Brockhaus, 1888.
*Giles, Herbert A.: *Confucianism and Its Rivals.* London, Williams and Norgate; New York, Scribner, 1915.
———: *A History of Chinese Literature.* London, Heinemann, 1901.
Granet, Marcel: *Chinese Civilization.* Translated by K. E. Innes and Mabel R. Brailsford. London, Kegan Paul; New York, Knopf, 1930.
———: *La Pensée chinoise.* Paris, Renaissance du livre, 1934.
Grube, Wilhelm: *Geschichte der chinesischen Literatur.* Leipzig, Amelang, 1909.
Haas, Hans: *Das Spruchgut Kung-tse's und Lao-tse's in gedanklicher Zusammenordnung.* Leipzig, J. C. Heinrichs, 1920.
Hackmann, Heinrich: *Chinesische Philosophie.* Munich, E. Reinhardt, 1927.
———: *Der Zusammenhang zwischen Schrift und Kultur in China.* Munich, E. Reinhardt, 1928.
*Liu Wu-chi: *A Short History of Confucian Philosophy.* Harmondsworth and Baltimore, Penguin Books, 1955.
*Soothill, W. E.: *The Three Religions of China.* 2d ed. London and New York, Oxford University Press, 1923.
*Suzuki, Daisetz Teitaro: *A Brief History of Early Chinese Philosophy.* 2d ed. London, Probsthain, 1914.
*Waley, Arthur: *Three Ways of Thought in Ancient China.* London, Allen and Unwin, 1939.
Wilhelm, Richard: *Chinesische Philosophie.* Breslau, Ferdinand Hirt, 1929.
———: *Confucius and Confucianism.* Translated by G. H. and A. P. Danton. London, Kegan Paul; New York, Harcourt, Brace, 1931.
———: *Kung-tse: Leben und Werk.* Stuttgart, F. Frommanns Verlag, 1925.
———: *A Short History of Chinese Civilization.* Translated by Joan Joshua. London, Harrap; New York, Viking Press, 1929.
Zenker, Ernst Viktor: *Geschichte der chinesischen Philosophie.* 2 vols. Reichenberg, Gebr. Stiepel, 1926-7.

Jesus

SOURCES:

Bible: *The Holy Bible: Revised Standard Version Containing the Old and New Testaments.* New York, Thomas Nelson & Sons, 1953.

*James, Montague Rhodes, trans.: *The Apocryphal New Testament.* New York, Oxford University Press, 1924.

SECONDARY WORKS:

Bultmann, Rudolf: *Jesus and the Word,* trans. by Louise Pettibone Smith and Erminie Huntress. New York and London, Scribner, 1934.

Dibelius, Martin: *Jesus,* trans. by Charles B. Hedrick and Frederick C. Grant. Philadelphia, Westminster Press, 1949.

————: *The Message of Jesus Christ: the Tradition of the Early Christian Communities, Restored and Translated into German,* English trans. by Frederick C. Grant, New York, Scribner, 1939.

Schweitzer, Albert: *The Quest of the Historical Jesus: a Critical Study of Its Progress from Reimarus to Wrede,* trans. by William Montgomery. New York, Macmillan, 1948.

INDEX OF NAMES